Manic Depression Is Also Known as Bipolar Affective Disorder
Includes Symptom List
2017

AGENTS

in

MY BRAIN

HOW I CONTINUE TO SURVIVE TYPE-ONE MANIC DEPRESSION

BILL HANNON

ARCHWAY
PUBLISHING

This book is a work of non-fiction. Unless otherwise noted, the author and the publisher make no explicit guarantees as to the accuracy of the information contained in this book and in some cases, names of people and places have been altered to protect their privacy.

Archway Publishing books may be ordered through booksellers or by contacting:

Archway Publishing
1663 Liberty Drive
Bloomington, IN 47403
www.archwaypublishing.com
1 (888) 242-5904

Because of the dynamic nature of the Internet, any web addresses or links contained in this book may have changed since publication and may no longer be valid. The views expressed in this work are solely those of the author and do not necessarily reflect the views of the publisher, and the publisher hereby disclaims any responsibility for them.

Any people depicted in stock imagery provided by Thinkstock are models, and such images are being used for illustrative purposes only.
Certain stock imagery © Thinkstock.

ISBN: 978-1-4808-5163-4 (sc)
ISBN: 978-1-4808-5164-1 (e)

Library of Congress Control Number: 2017953669

Print information available on the last page.

Archway Publishing rev. date: 09/11/2017

Chapters 1, 7, 14, and 26 originally appeared in the first edition of *Agents in My Brain* by Bill Hannon (Open Court, 1997). Chapters 28, 29, and 30 in this second edition are completely new. The remaining chapters are substantially revised versions of the ones that appeared in the first edition.

The story you are about to read is true. The names of people and places and some other details have been changed in order to protect the privacy of my friends and family.

Contents

CHAPTER 1

KGB BLOODHOUNDS

My name is Bill Hannon. Like thousands and thousands of other type-one manic depressives, when I was extremely manic, I had the delusion that I was a CIA/ FBI agent. The "Save the World from Crime" delusion is common in American manic depressives because so many of the TV shows, movies, and news stories are about cops versus criminals. The idea that we should build more prisons was a ridiculous manic delusion that I don't believe now. Other American manic depressives think they are God, Jesus, the Pope, or the President. Egyptian manics might think they are King Tut.

Type-one manic depressives get delusions when they are manic. Delusions are ridiculous ideas or reactions drawn from normal sights and sounds. This is different from hallucinations, which are sights and sounds that are not really there. Type-two manic depressives don't get delusional, but they do get the other symptoms of mania, so it is sometimes a problem. Both types get badly depressed at times.

It was April 1981. I was a twenty-one-year-old college student at the University of Washington in Seattle (UW). I had been in touch with reality but had been depressed for the entire year before that. I had already had manic-depressive mood swings for over four years. I had been normal, happy, and healthy until I was seventeen. In my manic illness, I began a crusade to stop crime. My plan was to get the Washington State Legislature to build a lot more prisons and keep them completely full of criminals. In my manic confusion, I wrote a letter to the governor in which I intended to say something against violence. However, the letter was worded so poorly and incoherently that the recipients didn't know what the letter meant. They figured I was mentally ill and was speaking of violence. They couldn't tell if I was against violence or in favor of it. They thought the letter was possibly some sort of threat. A bit later, I decided that the FBI, CIA, and/or Secret Service had checked out my background so carefully that they realized I was a good guy, that the letter was not a threat, and that I was so law-abiding that they wanted me to be an FBI agent. I was that delusional—that out of touch with reality. Being manic, my judgment was way off. I didn't know that there was something wrong with me. I felt excited, happy, and energetic. However, my speech and writing were hard to understand. I sent a letter to Governor Evans, which was meant to say:

Dear Governor Evans,

We are all in too much danger. The penalty for attempted first-degree murder is only three years in prison. The penalties are way too short like this because there is a lack of prison space … Please build more prison space. Sincerely, Bill Hannon

Instead, my letter was hard to understand. My intent was just to describe the general situation in the state—namely, that anyone with a motive for violence might go ahead and commit a crime. However, my letter was incoherent. It was more like:

Dear Governor Evans,

Someone could kill you. You better build more prisons ... This is a matter of life and death! Sincerely, Bill Hannon

This looks alarming, but at the time I thought it was just fine because I wasn't thinking straight. I had been manic a year earlier for a four-month period. I wrote some strange letters to professors at that time. There were other references to violence that were misunderstood in those letters. I was trying to say something against violence, but one sentence did not lead to another, and my choice of wording was inaccurate. The inaccurate wording probably reminded the readers of the myth that mentally ill or confused people are often dangerous. This myth is widely believed in our society. The incoherence alone in my letter to the governor probably would have alarmed any reader who believed in the "mentally ill people are dangerous" myth. Add in the references to violence that they could not figure out, and the governor's security guards apparently interpreted my letter as some sort of threat. They sent some people around to ask questions about me. I didn't know about that until a week or so later. I was utterly surprised that they thought my letter was some sort of threat. I had thought my letter was a clear statement against violence and crime.

I had been a college student, doing a political science internship with a state legislator. When that internship with State Legislator Denslow ended, because the college quarter was over, I was free to lobby the other representatives about criminal justice legislation. I wanted to stop crime. I hoped for some legislation that would establish mandatory minimum prison sentences for each felony and also would create the necessary prison space. I talked to many representatives—Democrats who were basically against the idea and Republicans who were almost all in favor. The House and Senate were controlled by the Democrats. Governor

Evans was a Republican. The head of the House Appropriations Committee was named Steve Leroux. The Appropriations Committee was going to have a hearing on appropriations for prisons at the end of March. I hoped to get a chance to speak at that hearing. I had a presentation planned including this song that I wrote:

The whites kill the whites, and the whites kill the blacks, and the blacks kill the blacks, and the blacks kill the whites, and the green grass grows all around, all around, and the green grass grows all around.

The point of my song was that something needed to be done about all the killing. We shouldn't just sit back and accept it. Also, too many of the Democratic legislators seemed to be saying that if I wanted to put criminals in prison, then I wanted to put blacks in prison, and therefore I was a racist. The Democrats seemed to be saying that criminals should be forgiven if they commit a crime and they're black. This never made sense, especially because black criminals usually have black victims. Most crimes in Washington State are committed by whites, and race should have nothing to do with sentencing. My idea that I could convince the whole legislature to do something—all by myself—was a grandiose delusion. My mania led me to falsely believe that Representative Leroux really would let me speak at the Appropriations Committee hearing. I called four television stations and two newspapers and told them to be at the hearing. I planned to be a big splash on the evening news. I even mailed out postcards to lots of people I had known, saying I was running for Congress in 1980. Being unrealistically optimistic was a symptom of mania. This was the third time in my life that I experienced a freaky and very severe manic episode. I had been normal until I was seventeen-and-a-half years old. Being manic feels very good. It is very exciting and fun, even though it is bizarre. The criminal justice appropriations hearing took place on April 3, 1981. One of the television stations

I had called was there, and there was a bunch of people testifying. Representative Denslow had said I was going to be on the agenda, but when I got there the agenda that he made up did not have my name on it. I was annoyed. I was hyper because I was manic. The hearing started, and people talked about a replacement for the women's prison because the current one wasn't adequate. I began to distribute my handouts. The handouts compared the cost of prisons with the cost of crime. I thought prisons were inexpensive compared with crime. My handouts had my suggestions for the minimum penalties that people should serve for all the various crimes. I was moving around a lot at the meeting to pass out my literature, while people were testifying to the committee. I'm sure now that was against the rules.

Also, when I was seated, I kept trying to see Leroux through a narrow aisle, which was my only view of him. He kept leaning one way or another. I was just trying to see him in order to pay attention to him when he was talking. Later I learned that somebody thought I was looking for a path to rush Leroux and attack him.

Also, I know that I looked nervous because at the beginning somebody told me so. I was just nervous about speaking and from being manic. Of course, I didn't realize that I was manic. I thought I could personally convince the state legislature to build a new five-thousand cell maximum security prison for the state by addressing the committee that day. I was out of touch with reality, and I didn't know it. It was fun and exciting. I was proud of the great knowledge I thought I had about how to stop crime.

When time was nearly up at the hearing, I yelled out from the audience, "Representative Leroux, you said I could speak. How about a chance?"

Everyone just ignored me. Later, I was near Representative Denslow's office, and he told me that one of the governor's bodyguards had been around asking questions about me.

He asked, "What did you say in that letter?"

I said, "Well I wrote, 'Your life is in danger from all the crime.'"

"Well, it was poor judgment to say 'Your life is in danger.'"

"Yeah, I guess."

That was the end of that discussion.

Later that night, my dad came over and said, "Bill, I've got to talk to you."

I said, "Let me guess. You got a call from the FBI?"

My dad said, "No. No. I got a call from Dean Carlson (Commissioner of Prisons). He said you were at some legislative meeting acting in a disturbed manner."

I said, "Really?"

"Yes, they thought you were going to rush the chairman."

"Rush him?" I said surprised.

"Yes."

"Rush him? That's ridiculous."

He said, "Look, I want you to go see Dr. Dan Holley. He's younger than Dr. Kelly [the psychiatrist I was seeing then], and he can help you."

I said, "Okay, okay, okay. I will."

I didn't argue, because I knew I had already accidentally annoyed the governor's bodyguards, and it wouldn't hurt to see another psychiatrist on an outpatient basis. My dad gave me Dr. Holley's phone number.

I called the number my dad gave me to make an appointment, and they made a point of getting me in the next day. I went to see Dr. Holley in his office and decided that he was not only a psychiatrist but also an agent for the FBI or CIA.

He talked to me for a little bit and then said, "I have a drug I want you to try."

I told him I didn't do drugs other than my mood leveler, lithium, and I wasn't interested.

He convinced me to take the prescription slip. I had been on the mood leveler lithium for a full year because I had been tentatively diagnosed with manic depression a year earlier at the age of twenty. Obviously, the lithium was not working too well at this point. When I left his office, I went to a bookstore to look the prescription up in *The Physicians' Desk Reference.* The name of the drug was spelled "Sineguan" on the prescription slip that Holley had filled out. I looked it up and found an entry for an antidepressant called Sinequan. Obviously, the *g* should have been a *q* on the slip. I took this misspelling as a hint that I was not really supposed to take the drug being prescribed. I looked at the list of side effects, and one of them was hallucinations. I decided that Dr. Holley had prescribed this drug as an FBI trick. I thought the FBI knew I would look up the side effects. I thought they wanted to see if I would deliberately induce hallucinations in myself, so that I would have a defense for murder. I thought they wanted to see if I would try to use the insanity defense. Hallucinations show insanity. I was really paranoid. I had the unrealistic fear that the FBI was watching me and playing this dirty trick on me. They couldn't arrest me, because I hadn't done anything. So, I imagined they were pulling dirty tricks on me. I didn't get the misspelled prescription for Sinequan filled. I'm not a murderer, and I didn't want hallucinations. I know now that it was just as well that I didn't take the Sinequan, because it would've probably made my symptoms worse. It was an antidepressant, not an antipsychotic for mania, the manic stage of the disease. In reality, it wasn't a trick; it was just an erroneous and misspelled prescription. Over the next several days I lost touch with reality further. I still had no insight into my situation. I thought I was fine, but I really wasn't. For example, I was reading the University of Washington student newspaper. In the paper, there is a classified section for fraternities and sororities. There are usually ads in there like, "Hey Jim and Dave of Sigma Delta Phi, thanks for the great time Monday. Love, your little sisters Stacy, Sandy, Angie, Sue, Dawn, Jane, Laurie and Mary."

Well, being manic, I started to think that all those ads were directed at me. I thought of anyone I had ever known with those girls' first names, and I figured they had all gotten together to get in touch with me. I was ecstatic. For one thing, they were probably in love with me. For another, they had probably heard about my plans to run for Congress and wanted to work on my campaign. I felt very flattered.

After awhile, I thought the FBI and CIA had realized that their concern about my letter was completely unfounded. I figured they realized I was a good guy. I thought they had checked me out carefully and had found that I was very law-abiding. I had even reached the rank of Eagle in Boy Scouts.

I also developed delusions about music. I thought the choice of songs on the radio—and sometimes the actual words of songs being played—were being altered by the FBI or CIA to have a special meaning for me. I figured that my car was bugged, my house was bugged, my phone was tapped, my mail was being opened, and I was being followed. By now, though, I thought it was not being done to guard against something bad I might do but instead so that the FBI could keep track of what I was doing. By keeping track of what I was doing, the FBI would best be able to help me get elected to Congress. I was overjoyed. They wanted to get me elected because they had figured out that I was tough on crime. I was not violent. I wanted to stop violence. They couldn't overtly help me, because as federal employees they couldn't get involved in politics—I thought. So, they had to help me covertly. This was all according to my grandiose delusions. The fact that my house was bugged (or so I thought), let them know what radio station I was listening to, so they could alter words of songs to give me secret messages.

In a few days, I had another appointment with Dr. Holley. I forget exactly what he said, but I remember he told me he had been a lieutenant colonel (a high rank) in the air force during the Vietnam War. I decided he was still in the air force intelligence branch and was my commanding officer. The intelligence community would help get me elected to Congress. It was very exciting. I told him I was going down to Tacoma to visit my friends at the University of Puget Sound (UPS). I had gone to school there for my first two years.

He said, "Take my card along, and give me a call if you run into any trouble."

I went down to UPS about nine o'clock at night. I thought a whole caravan of cars was following me down there. I got to UPS and went to the house of some friends. They had just gone to sleep when I got there, but I had called so they knew I was coming. One of their roommates was gone, so I tried to sleep in his bed. I think I just lay there a few hours. Then I got up and started looking for my shoes. After some trouble finding my shoes, during which I woke one of my friends, I went out and drove around for a while. Then I came back to their house and sat in the living room for the rest of the night. My mind was filled with great, fun, optimistic thoughts. It was exciting to be running for Congress, and to feel so good, instead of being depressed. I didn't realize that I was out of my mind. This was a manic phase of manic depression.

I had had two previous manic episodes since age seventeen-and-a-half, but since then, I had mostly been depressed. It felt good to sit in my friends' living room and make great, optimistic plans. The next day, my friends in that house got sick of me, and they sent me over to Jewish House where I knew a couple of people. Jewish House was a residential house for Jews on campus who wanted to keep kosher and observe other Jewish traditions. I guess Tim, one of the guys there, was writing a story and needed a new character.

One of my friends in the first house later sent over a note saying, "This is your new character," I guess meaning me.

I didn't really notice. I was too busy talking to them, trying to pick up secret coded information from them, and give other information to them. It was fun. I thought I was finally doing something fun and exciting on this campus rather than hanging out in my dorm room being depressed. Before I dropped out, that's what I did. I hung out in my dorm room and was depressed.

As I talked to the people in Jewish House, I jumped from topic to topic, I'm sure. I remember I kept doing an imitation of an Israeli trying to speak English: "I eh, don' know. Eh, how do you say in English?"

Also, I kept throwing my head to one side like you do when you first lift your head out of a pool to get water out of your eyes. Swimming lives on in my mind when I feel good. I enjoyed being on the swim team when I was healthy in high school.

At Jewish House, there was a poster on the wall that said, "Consider Yourself One of the Committed."

Of course, this meant committed to Judaism, but I kept thinking it could mean being committed to a mental hospital because my dad had been saying that I was nuts. It was a suspicious poster.

I thought my car had been stolen. Eventually I found out I had just forgotten where I parked it. The people I had been talking to at Jewish House were Tim and Rita, and I told them I thought my car had been stolen. Tim wanted to call campus security, but I told him not to. Later when I was out walking around, Tim called campus security. I think he reported that I was acting strange and that I didn't want to call them when my car had been stolen.

That evening I was in the student union, and a group of campus security guards came up to me and asked, "Are you Bill Hannon?"

I said, "Yes."

They asked, "What are you on this campus for?" (I had dropped out of UPS a year earlier, and I was now attending UW.)

"I cannot say."

Then they started pushing me and asked, "Why can't you say?"

"I cannot say why I cannot say, and quit pushing me or I'll get you guys arrested."

"What for?"

"Assault."

"Well, we think you're on campus to threaten a professor."

"No."

A few minutes later they left me alone. I had written anticrime letters to some professors during my manic episode a year earlier. The problems with the 1980 letters to professors arose from my misunderstood references to violence. This was the same problem I had just repeated in the 1981 letters to the governor. Being manic makes a person impossible to understand. People can get the meaning exactly backward. The likelihood of misunderstanding is increased by the abundance in the media of misconceptions about mental illness. Too often, mental illness only makes the news when some killer is pleading insanity. Most people arrested on suspicion of murder are perfectly sane and perfectly guilty. On the other hand, most mentally ill people are perfectly peaceful. They are two different groups. Criminals, in their desperate attempt to stay out of jail, end up slandering and libeling mentally ill people by saying they are one of us. They only wish.

Sometime later, after talking to the security guards, I was out walking around campus. Rita called my high school friend David Frish, and my psychiatrist, Dr. Holley. I had given her their names and phone numbers because I thought she was CIA also. I guess she told them I was crazy.

I spent the evening wandering around campus, looking at the things people had written on their dorm room doors, thinking that the writing contained secret messages to me or about me. I thought I should send some secret messages as well as receive them.

I thought the song "Dirty Water" had to be sung to one particular girl, so I knocked on her door and started singing it.

She said, "Bill, I don't know what you are talking about."

So, I left. I was also looking for Brett Pritchard's house. He lived in a college-owned house, the address of which I didn't know. The campus directory just gave the name of the house. I was going to speak to him about the fight against crime. His father was a congressman. That evening, I also crashed a few parties that were going on in dorms. I just walked in. I stayed for just a minute because I thought I was on a secret mission that I couldn't tell anyone about, and then I left. Around ten thirty or so at night, I went back to Jewish House and told them I was going to stay there and sleep. I had prearranged to stay in the room of a friend there because he was out of town. He was a friend of mine from my dorm floor freshman year. I was getting into bed, but first when I was stumbling around his room, I accidentally unplugged his clock radio. When I plugged it back in, it blinked 12:00. I didn't know why it did that. I thought it was another clue. Twelve midnight is the witching hour. Witches are criminals and should be punished.

I started singing, "Ding dong the witch is dead," and I started sweeping with a broom I had found because witches ride broomsticks.

Then Rita said I was making too much noise, so I left. Then I decided that the whole campus was a CIA training base and that everybody was supposed to switch dorm rooms to confuse the KGB, the Soviet Union's spy agency. I went to the lounge of a dorm and watched the late night Associated Press news on television. The news was printed on the screen and would gradually scroll up. I blinked a few times—or several times—after reading each word or sentence. I thought the CIA could tell what I was reading by shining lasers through the TV screen into my eyes and back to the television. Of course, I thought the information was coded secrets. For example, some of the news was about the National Long Course Swimming Championships. When it got to the breaststroke, I thought they were telling me that if I did well on this mission, it would make up for all the bad breaststroke races I had participated in. I thought this was all very exciting and fun. I thought I was very clever. It was good to have a sense of purpose.

I stayed in the dorm lounge for a while, and then I left and went walking around campus. A small cocker spaniel started following me. At first I thought nothing of it, but then I thought it was sent to trail me by the KGB. It probably had a microscopic radio-transmitting device on its collar. So, in keeping with the delusion that everyone on campus was supposed to switch dorm rooms to confuse the KGB, and in keeping with the delusion that the dog was trailing my scent for the KGB, I did what people do in the movies when bloodhounds are chasing them. I crossed water. It washes off the scent. The dogs lose your trail. That way the KGB wouldn't be able to capture me. I took off my jacket, shirt, shoes, and socks, and I swam across a pond on campus that had a dormitory on the other side. I stopped in the middle to pour mud on my head. I thought, *This is a crazy way to make a living.* I wondered if being a CIA agent was enough to impress Melanie Carson, a woman I had a huge crush on in high school.

I kept thinking about the song that has the line, "Save my life I'm going down for the last time." I pretended to have trouble swimming as I thought of those lyrics. I had no trouble swimming, but it was cold. It was April 12 in Tacoma, Washington. It was about 6:00 a.m. when I got out of the pond and ran into the dorm and into the men's showers. I took a hot shower to warm up. So far, nobody had seen me. After about ten minutes in the shower, I got out. I walked down the hall and saw someone's name written on his door. It was "Brewster." "Ster" was a syllable that reminded me of a nickname I used to have. The door was unlocked, so I walked in. There was nobody there. I used a towel to dry off, and I changed into some dry underwear that I found in a drawer. It fit. Then I put on some pants and a shirt, and they fit. I thought I had arrived at my new address, the one I was supposed to go to in order to confuse the KGB. I read the class schedule of the room's occupant, and then I started reading his letters from home. I figured I would have to take on his identity. I was getting comfortable and even turned on a radio. Soon the real occupant of the room came back. (He had been watching the space shuttle launch down the hall.)

He asked, "What are you doing in my room?"

I said, "It's my room now."

He said, "No, it's my room."

"We're all supposed to switch rooms. Go over to Jewish House, and they will tell you about this."

"You're wearing my clothes."

"No. They're my clothes."

"No. They're mine," he said angrily, throwing his arms up in the air. "Oh, God."

"Go over to the Jewish House, and they'll explain this to you," I said.

He said, "No," with an angry look on his face.

I said, "Well, then call the police." I thought the police would side with me.

He called campus security, who then called the police.

They got Dr. Holley on the walkie-talkie phone link, and I heard him say, "Yeah, he's a psycho."

They handcuffed me and drove me up to McCormick hospital in Seattle. As I got out of the police car at McCormick hospital, I faked an epileptic seizure, but the cops just grabbed me and brought me up to the psychiatric ward. When I got onto the psychiatric ward, I tried to figure out who was CIA and who was not. I also tried to figure out who was a Pacific Lutheran University (PLU) alumnus and who was a UPS alumnus. I thought there was a friendly rivalry within the CIA between the two schools since they were in the same town, Tacoma.

I acted bizarrely for several days while I was in the hospital. I tried to talk in code. Code, I thought, was usually made up of words that had double meanings. However, I immediately agreed to take medication because I thought Dr. Holley was my commanding officer in the CIA, and he said I should take it. He said that I would get out of the hospital quickly if I took the medication. He also said I was schizophrenic. Feeling that that was a serious illness, I decided to take the medication. Of course, deciding that I was schizophrenic was incorrect but not so surprising at this particular point because when someone is acutely manic, it's hard to tell if they're acutely manic or schizophrenic. The treatments for the acute stages are similar. As I look back over my medical records, I see that I was given the treatment for mania (the manic phase of manic depression) while I was in the hospital. I had been on the mood leveler lithium, the most common treatment for manic depression back then, and I hadn't missed a dose. Dr. Holley continued the lithium and gave me the antipsychotic medication, Thorazine, in addition to the antipsychotic medication, Prolixin. Medication eventually proves to be the hero of this book. Gradually, I got better. Slowly I realized that the hospital was not a rest and relaxation haven for CIA agents. At first I wrote a lot of irrelevant notes to be put on my chart, and then I gradually quit writing them. Eventually I wrote postcards to some of the people I had told that I was running for Congress.

In the postcards, I said, "Sorry for bugging you. I'm in a psychiatric ward diagnosed with schizophrenia. My running for Congress was a strange delusion."

I was well enough to realize that I had been crazy.

I was in the hospital for about three weeks. The antipsychotic medication made me catch up on sleep, which helped me a lot. After about a week, my delusions were gone, and they transferred me to the open ward. There were therapy groups, where we sat in a circle and talked, recreation groups, where we played games, and occupational therapy, which is better described as arts and crafts. When I started to get better, my high school poker friends started calling me and visiting me at the hospital. They lived in Seattle and we were still friends four years after high school.

In the upcoming months of June and July 1981, two of my friends, Jim Eckhart and Jack Johnson, were getting married to their girlfriends of several years. On one of the last days I was in the hospital, at the end of April, Jim, Jack, Phil Holland, Stan Gold, Dave Frish, and I met and discussed plans for a stag party we would throw for Jim and Jack. Having morals, we opted for a clean stag, where we would just have dinner and play poker.

CHAPTER 2

HEALTHY, OPTIMISTIC HIGH SCHOOL

The previous chapter described a manic episode I experienced during what should have been my senior year of college. I had been happy, healthy, and normal my whole life up through eleventh grade and the first part of twelfth grade in 1975 and 1976. Often since then, I have compared things to how I was in eleventh grade. I do this in order to see how far away I am from there or to figure out what the healthy me would have done lately, or should do right now. The years 1975 and 1976 were the standard for conduct and thought against which I judged myself when I was depressed in later years. I still suffer from manic depression to this day, but I am much better. I don't judge myself as much. Things are more acceptable in the present.

As I'm writing this second edition of this book, it is now the year 2017. Over the past few years, I've gotten good medical treatment. I don't refer to the past healthy me as much in order to know what to do. I mostly know what to do.

During eleventh grade, life seemed really nice and beautiful. I was still super-jock, super-brain, and super-smooth compared to how I am now. Manic depression had not struck yet, and life was normal and fun.

I had always just assumed I would be healthy until I was sixty five. I had never heard of manic depression. During eleventh grade, school and surrounding activities were easy and fun for me. As one of my extracurricular activities, I served as treasurer for Jewish Teen Group (JTG). During the summer before eleventh grade, I ran our chapter because the president, Stan Gold, was in Israel. Stan Gold was a good friend of mine. We had been friends since seventh grade, and he was one of the guys I played poker with on weekends. Our adult youth group leader in JTG was Darren Gollub. He had been impressed with my leadership abilities that summer.

Besides spending time with the youth group, I was also working out for swimming and doing my homework. I had decided to try to get straight As, even if it meant having to do some homework. In junior high, I had a very simple policy; I didn't do homework and I got straight As. That practice had worked in seventh through ninth grade, but tenth grade showed me that homework was necessary in senior high.

I socialized with a group of poker friends. We had been playing together on weekends, a couple times a month, since Christmas vacation in tenth grade. We had been friends for years. We had gone to Mercer Island Junior High together. We had gone to Mercer Island Senior High together. Many of us had gone to grade school, Hebrew school, JTG, Sunday school, and Boy Scouts together. We were a tight-knit group that had in common honesty, responsibility, some athletic ability, and academic ability. We really enjoyed each other's company. We played a lot of different poker games and other card games, and we had our own slang for much of it. "BHGMFNPW" stood for 'Beacon Hill Guts, Mit Fours, Natch Pair Walks," which meant, "The guts game taught to us by our friend from Beacon Hill where the low card in your hand is wild, fours are always wild, and a pair not involving wild cards is necessary to win the pot if you are unopposed."

A "criker" was a hand that tended to drive you up a creek without a paddle if you played it wrong. We would deal the cards and then go around the table stating whether we were in or out. If you said "GTBITB," it meant: "Got to be in there boys." "Trout," meant you were out. The games were exciting, and people would miss games only if they had a date or had to work. Everyone paid their IOU's.

As a high school student, I was naturally living with my family. Let me try to explain them. My dad's name is Lee, and he was forty-eight years old when I was in eleventh grade. My mom was named Nancy and was forty-five. I had an older brother, Steve, who was eighteen. I had a younger brother, Rick, who was thirteen, and a brother Johnny who was eight.

My dad didn't want me to date from 1971 through 1975, when I was age twelve through age sixteen. I can only speculate as to why. I guess, projecting backward, my dad wanted me to hang around with him instead of going out on dates.

I didn't really date anyone during those years, but whenever I told my dad that I was with a group of guys and girls at someone's house, he said angrily, "What were you doing over there?"

"We were talking."

"Well, what were you doing over there?"

"Um, ah, we were talking," I would say, and then I would tiptoe on to another topic.

In the fall of 1976, my dad's attitude problem became much worse. He got very lonely and jealous, as I'll describe in more detail in chapter 4 below. The cause of my dad's loneliness during the years 1971 to 1975 must have been my mom's manic depression. My mom, Nancy, suffered from manic depression from 1955, the same year that she and my father got engaged, up until she died in 1981. My mom was often sad, distracted, irritable, worried, tearful, dependent, and slow-thinking.

This had to be from the depressed phase of manic depression. This would be bad enough to make my dad unhappy in his marriage to my mom. I think it made him want to hang around with me. I did not know my mom had a disease. My parents never told me. Any diagnosis of her had been very vague. We thought the way she behaved was normal for her, and we were used to it. She didn't seem that much different from other mothers. However, because my mom was less fun than she should have been, my dad wanted attention from me. That is why he didn't want me to date and instead wanted me to hang around with him. This is my theory. However, on January 2, 1975, January of my tenth-grade year, things got worse. My mom had a stroke. She lost her ability to walk, talk, read, and write. Her right side was paralyzed.

She could only say, "Dee, deeee, dee. De, dee, dee," in sentences. She could still shake her head, "Yes" or "No."

As a result of my mom's stroke in January, there was an even greater potential for my dad to want me to stick by him. He eventually wanted me to dump everyone else. He wanted companionship. He was married to my crippled mother, which was a horrible strain.

My mom's stroke did not cause me to be depressed or manic at that time. I was a healthy tenth-grader in the fall of 1974. During that time my mom was often irritable as a result of her poorly diagnosed and almost completely untreated manic depression. They couldn't give her medication for manic depression, because she had a heart condition, which could have been made worse by the medication. She would often yell at me for no reason.

Perversely, the stroke turned out to be a somewhat positive thing for me at first. One of the effects of her stroke was that she was left unable to speak, so she was unable to yell. So, at that time, I felt her stroke wasn't completely bad, and I tried to look on the bright side of the situation.

My childhood was happy. I never had a trace of manic depression myself. My childhood memories are mostly good. When I was younger, even my moody mom was a good mother. I knew she loved me, and she did nice things for me. She talked to me about my day, bought me clothes that I liked, bought me green grapes, signed me up for activities, supervised me, and guided me through life.

She really didn't yell at me much when I was little. We got along. I was glad she was home when I got home from school.

She often said, "Have I told you lately that I love you?"

I said, "Yes, Mom. I love you, too," and I hugged her.

When I was little, my dad was also a good dad. He taught me how to play baseball, how to build radios, and how to fish. He taught me how to behave.

I had a happy childhood. There is a study that proves that manic depression is not related to any abnormalities in personality before the illness sets in. For that reason, I will not go into depth about my childhood. I was happy and well-adjusted as a kid. The study of personality looked at thousands of healthy nineteen-year-olds. These were nineteen-year-olds who had never experienced any psychiatric illness in their lives. The researchers looked at the ones who became manic depressive years later. They looked back at the records of how the manic depressives had been when they were healthy and nineteen. The researchers concluded that the manic depressives' personalities when they were healthy did not differ from those who had remained healthy. I was healthy and happy as a child and adolescent. I didn't get manic depression until I was seventeen. Details of my childhood are irrelevant.

I'll get back to high school. The way I see it now, it was my mom's depressed and irritable mood that made us fail to get along during fall of tenth grade. Before the stroke, she would occasionally scream because I would speak in the wrong tone of voice.

She would call me for breakfast and say, "Biiiiiiellllllll."

I would say, "Whaaaaaaaattttttt?"

Then she would get really mad at me for mocking her. She would yell, "You listen to me. Don't you mock me. Don't let me ever hear you talk in that mimicking tone of voice. Do you understand me?"

I'd say, "Yes, Mom."

I was getting yelled at for using the wrong tone of voice. I know now that the times when she was most depressed were the times when my parents would go into their room, shut the door, and argue.

Then my dad would tell us, "Mother feels bad, so be nice to her."

Also, after the birth of each of my two younger brothers, she stayed in the hospital for a while because she "felt bad," or so we were told. I know now that she was in the hospital for either postpartum mania or depression. We weren't allowed to visit her. Manic depression has a large genetic component. I got the genes for it from my mother.

When my mom had her stroke on January 2, 1975, I was in tenth grade. I wanted her to get better so that she wouldn't suffer. Also, I knew that if my mom got better, my dad would act normally and not act like a pest, the way my widowed grandmother sometimes did. I figured that being widowed was like being married to someone very crippled. I figured this caused people to bug their kids. My dad was nearly widowed because my mom was so crippled from the stroke. My dad was in a worse situation than most widowers. He couldn't date because my mom was still half alive. Also, it was just awful to see that my mom could go from healthy to crippled so quickly. It was terrible to know that we would have to live with her suffering and try to help her, even though helping her was so futile. We couldn't make her better. At temple when we said the mourner's prayer, I felt like we were saying it for my mom, but I didn't get depressed until almost two years later—in November of 1976, when I was in twelfth grade.

Mom could just say, "Dee, de, deee, de, deee," in sentences. We could ask her yes or no questions, and she would shake or nod her head. Sometimes her tone of voice, expression on her face, or gestures with her good left arm were clues.

She'd say, "De, deee, dee, de, dee, dee, deee," pointing west.

We'd guess, "Something about Dad?"

She'd shake her head "No," and say, "Dee."

We'd guess, "Something about John?"

She'd nod, and say, "Dee."

We'd guess, "He's at the Felbers?"

She'd nod her head "Yes," and say "Dee."

Many times, it was much tougher, and often, we never figured out what she meant.

The good thing was she could still dress herself and go to the bathroom herself.

In spite of my mother's illnesses, Dad was still easy to get along with during eleventh grade. He was a commercial real estate agent, and he made a good living. That year he went to work and didn't bother me. He hired a household helper to come during the day to help with my mom, the housework, and my little brother, Johnny. Johnny was in third grade. My brother, Steve, was a freshman in college and lived away from home. Steve had at first been very upset by my mother's stroke and had hesitated to go away to college for his freshman year because of it. He felt bad about leaving Dad and Mom just eight months after the stroke. However, he knew he couldn't really help her, and so he reluctantly went off to college. My brother Rick was in eighth grade. He was upset about Mom's situation but was gradually adjusting to the idea as well as he could. I really only saw Johnny, Rick, and my parents during dinner. I ate quickly, and then I went and did my homework. I pretty much ignored Mom.

During the fall of junior year, Dad approved of my activities. These were the JTG youth group, homework, poker, and some pre-season swim workouts, which kept me busy. The official swim season started November 15, with practice one hour before school and two hours after. It was a real strain, but it was what we had to do to become successful swimmers. My personal goal was to earn a letter, so I could wear a letter jacket and be known as a great athlete. Traditionally, one had to be in the top twelve in regions to letter. I swam the 50-yard breaststroke in the medley relay and the individual 100-yard breaststroke. Swimming worked out really well in eleventh grade. The positive experience of swimming is one of the memories that would come to mind later during my manic highs. The following year, my swimming ability was to be the first casualty of my manic depression. You can't swim well when you are depressed and unable to concentrate.

In the middle of my eleventh-grade swimming season, two great things happened. My first-semester report card arrived bearing straight As, even for the honors classes I was taking. The second great thing that happened in January was that the change in semester put Melanie Carson in my physics class. She was one of the best-looking girls in the school, and she sat right next to me. She was half Asian, with long, straight, shiny dark brown hair and a perfect face. She was so beautiful that I had looked her up in the yearbook back in eighth grade to find out what her name was. She had never been in any of my classes, even though we had gone to the same school since seventh grade. Now I finally had a chance to get to know her. This was a fantasy come true. Melanie was a lead singer in a local rock n' roll band. She was a good singer and was popular around school because of it. In contrast to the wild rock n' roller image she portrayed on stage, she was known to be pretty straitlaced, and she hung out with some of the best athletes at school. Melanie Carson would have been a great girlfriend. The following year, she did go out with me once. Later, she was to become a depressive obsession. At that later time, when I was very depressed, I would think that only hugs and kisses from her could cheer me up.

I swam to impress girls like Melanie. I figured that when I got really good, I could invite girls to meets, and I could show off. I thought Melanie and others admired great athletes. I swam the 100-yard breaststroke at a time of 1:13.5 or so at most of our meets that year. The last meet for me that year was the regional meet. If I placed in the top twelve, I would letter and be able to wear a letter jacket. When my heat came up in regions, I walked to the end of the pool with the starting blocks. The guys from the previous heat got out of the pool and walked by me dripping wet and breathing heavily. The starter said, "Swimmers up."

We got up on the starting blocks. I curled my toes over the edge. "Take your marks." I bent over and grabbed the starting block. Bang! I dove in the water and swam as hard as I could. I remember pushing myself to swim even harder. By the third length I could see an opponent to my right out of the corner of my eye. I kept going, and my hands and quadriceps started to hurt like they were supposed to. I pushed myself to the end. At the end, I rammed my fingertips into the wall to stop the clock. Much to my surprise, my time was 1:10.12. My best time ever. Being relaxed and rested from easier practices at the end of the season helped like they were supposed to. I came in tenth, so I lettered. I was quite proud of myself.

During physics class on Monday I said to my friend Dave, loud enough for Melanie to hear, "The swim season is almost over, I'm not a superstar, but I did letter."

Then it was springtime, and I didn't need to swim anymore until the next year, and I could buy a letter jacket. I was happy. I was very happy.

Honors Physics was not too hard, but we had to pay close attention in class. This left no time to talk to Melanie, but just sitting next to her was thrilling enough so that physics was fun. Even when we had a minute to talk, I could never think of anything to say, so I'd end up talking to Dave. I also managed to talk to Melissa, Melanie's lab partner, a little bit more than to Melanie. I figured both Melanie and Melissa had boyfriends.

I am now a long way from being in shape like I was then. The medication used to treat manic depression has had side effects including increased hunger. The hunger has made me gain weight. In eleventh grade, I was 5' 9" and 145 pounds. I now weigh 220 pounds and am the same height.

In order for me to become a great swimmer for the next season and be the number one breaststroker on our team, I figured I had to swim under 1:07.0 in twelfth grade. Then, I could also make it to the state meet and be a star. There was a summer Amateur Athletic Union (AAU) season that I could swim in. Plus, I could run and lift weights. Doing these things over the summer could help me excel during the varsity season in the winter of my senior year.

Doing this was in apparent conflict with the alternative for me for that summer, which was being a camp counselor in training (CIT) at the camp I had attended the previous year, Camp Okransky. I had been hired as a CIT back in November. It was a big honor to be hired because the counselor-in-training positions were hard to get. It would be a lot of fun, and it would be a better atmosphere for a social life and love life because there would be a lot of female staff. Staying home and swimming would make me a great swimmer for my senior year but would not give me as good a social life during the summer.

To help me decide what to do, I called my counselors from camp the previous year and asked them what to do.

They all said, "Go to camp."

One said, "You can swim at camp."

I thought, *Yeah right, no coach, no teammates, no wall for flip turns, screaming kids in the way, and algae-infested lake water. Also, no stopwatches, no meets, not enough sleep, not enough time, cold weather, huge waves, and no moral support for swimming.*

I called the head of the CITs to ask her what we would be doing as CITs at camp. She was an attractive woman, and she was married to the camp director. They were both in their early twenties. I had met them at a group interview. Her husband was a long-distance runner. He ran 5,000-meter races just for fun. I described my dilemma.

She seemed very friendly, and she said, "You can swim at camp."

I said, "Well, it is really tough to practice in a lake."

"We'll have a really big beach area. Our waterfront is going to be twenty yards across."

"Twenty?"

"Yeah."

"Oh, uh, and how deep?"

"Well, it's going to be real gradual. There will be a beginner and an advanced beginner section that goes up to three-and-a-half feet. Then an intermediate part that goes up to four-and-a-half feet, and then our swimmers area that I think will go up to nine feet," she said in a concerned, sweet, caring voice.

I really liked talking to her and she seemed to want me to come up there. Nobody as nice as she was telling me directly to swim in the AAU season. I thought it refreshing to see such a young, athletically inclined, well-adjusted couple who were legally married. They were good role models.

"Will there be time to swim?" I asked.

She said, "You get one free activity period each day, and there is free time for an hour every day. How much do you have to swim?"

"Well, at home I'd be swimming four hours per day."

"Would it be okay if you swam only two hours?"

"It would be okay, I said, "but not as good. Tell me a little more about what we are going to do."

She gave me some more information. I told her I would call her back in a couple of days and tell her my decision.

Next I called Joel Stein. He had been selected to be a CIT and was also an athlete. He played football and baseball at a different high school nearby. He had been a camper in my cabin the previous summer. He knew how to get what he wanted out of life, and I trusted his judgment.

I said, "I'm thinking about swimming this summer in the AAU season at home. I could even win districts and make it to state next year in my event, if I swim this summer."

He said, "Camp will be fun, you should come to camp. Some fine women are going to be there."

We discussed which women would be there. We had some mutual acquaintances.

I asked, "Do you think I should go?"

"Does your coach want you to stay?"

"Well, it would be better."

"Do you have a girlfriend who wants you to stay?"

"No."

"Oh, just come to camp. Do you know what? The head of the CITs said that during prep week we will go to a drive-in movie in a bus and turn the bus sideways so that we can all see. Isn't that a riot?"

I said, "Yeah, I s'pose."

"Don't you think it would be fun to go to a drive-in movie in a bus, and turn the bus sideways?"

"Yeah, sounds kind of fun."

"C'mon, Bill. It'll be fun. You can swim after camp."

We talked for a while.

At the end of the conversation I said, "Joel, thanks for your opinion. I'm going to think about it awhile."

He said, "Okay, I hope you come. Bye."

"Bye."

I thought it over and decided I'd do it as long as I could swim 3000 yards per day. That should have taken an hour and fifteen minutes, if I did a lot of breaststroke.

I called the head of the CITs and told her I would go, as long as I could swim an hour and fifteen minutes a day. She said that was doable, and so I said I'd see her there. I would put up with the algae, no coach, no clock, no wall, and no meets, etc.

Other things were happening that Spring of eleventh grade besides my debate on being a CIT. The eleventh-grade swim season had ended in early March. After that, I had much more free time. While I did a couple of JTG things, I actually started studying even more. I wanted to be able to get into any college. I wanted to have the option of going away to Harvard, Yale, Stanford, or The University of Puget Sound. It took good grades to get into those places, and I wanted to graduate from high school with distinction. We had gotten our Preliminary Scholastic Aptitude Test (PSAT) results back in the winter and I, along with almost everyone I played poker with, scored in the 99th percentile. I was a National Merit Commended Student. I was very proud of myself and my friends.

I studied more for all my classes once swimming was over that year. When it was warm and sunny, I studied outside and worked on my tan.

Meanwhile, I was making no progress with Melanie Carson. I could never think of anything to say to her, and there was no time to say it anyway. After every physics test, almost everyone would tell almost everyone else what score he or she got on the test. Melanie, however, would not tell me, even though she sat right next to me. However, she didn't show anyone else her test paper either. The only person she showed was her lab partner, Melissa. I didn't know if that was because she did well and was being modest, because she did lousy and was embarrassed, or if she was just being unfriendly. Her lab partner however, Melissa Jenkins, was friendly and had asked me to help her with her physics homework a few times in study hall. I gladly obliged. After school was over, before camp started, I asked Melissa out. Melissa agreed to go out with me.

We went to a movie and then had a pizza. I had fun on the date and was glad that I was out with someone of her intelligence, looks, status, and warmth.

I don't remember much of what we said; however, I remember sitting in my car outside her house afterward saying life was great and fun.

I said, "The biggest problem most people have is deciding what sport to go out for or who to ask out."

We kissed goodnight, and the date was over.

Now that I am manic-depressive, the euphoric manic mood reminds me often very intensely of this last half of eleventh grade, early twelfth grade, and the summer in-between. Normal good moods, like the moods I experienced then, didn't happen much after that.

I kept swimming and weightlifting right up until the day before camp. That was Tuesday, June 15th, 1976.

CHAPTER 3

CAMP: GOOD TIMES

I had a great time at Camp Okransky that summer. It was fun working with kids because they look up to you. I supervised campers in each of the three sessions, I taught swimming lessons, organized a tetherball tournament, swam laps an hour myself each day, and luckily, I started dating Angie Spiess. She was a real sweetie but kind of shy.

That summer of 1976 was the last summer that I was healthy. In later years, when I was in a manic high mood, I would be intensely and vividly reminded of the friends I had made, male and female, during that great summer of 1976, before my senior year of high school.

We learned some Jewish values. Romance is a "mitzvah" six days a week. "Mitzvah" is Hebrew for "commandment" or "good deed" which means it's something God wants you to do. Romance is a double mitzvah on the Sabbath. Sabbath is Friday night at sundown until Saturday night at sundown, and you get to sleep late Saturday morning. Also, Jewish values include the idea that contraception is allowed and that women are entitled to enjoy lovemaking.

CHAPTER 4

MY GREAT FALL FALLS APART

When I got home from camp, I called Angie. She called me back a couple of days later. We went out to eat. She told me about the classes she had that fall and about her tennis team. I talked about my classes and swimming. We talked about what movies we wanted to see, and she also mentioned a couple of Shakespearian plays she wanted to see. We talked about people from camp, too. I liked that she acted very mature and sophisticated.

Then, later on, each evening we went out, we parked in an empty parking lot and made out. It was enjoyable for me, but we were both very inexperienced in relationships. It was not very pleasurable for her. This hurt our relationship a lot.

Besides our inexperience, another problem was beginning to develop. My father was getting jealous of my relationship with Angie. I was surprised at the depth of his jealousy and anger. He was lonely because of my mother's condition.

On Saturday evenings, my dad would notice that I had taken a shower. Then, after I got dressed, he would barge into my room and start screaming at me. He would scream that Saturday nights were for the family to watch TV together. He yelled that I was wearing out my mom's car by driving to Angie's house. (My mom quit driving in January 1975 because of her stroke.)

I said, "Should I quit swimming and get a job to pay for the use of the car?"

"I don't want you to do that!" He yelled angrily.

I yelled, "Get out of my room!"

He would stay in my room and yell for another minute.

"*I* never had a girlfriend when *I was your age!*" He screamed.

I thought, *What a weirdo.*

Then I would yell, "Mom, tell Dad to get out of my room. Get out of my room!"

My Mom would say, "Dee deeee dee." By the tone of her voice, we could tell she was siding with me.

I would repeat, "Mom, tell Dad to get out of my room. Get out of my room!"

She repeated, "Deeeee, dee, dee."

Then, in a disgusted tone, my dad would say, "Oh, all right."

He would then get out of my room and say, "Do you need any money?"

I would say, "Yes. I need money for gas."

He'd give me five dollars, shake my hand, and say, "Have a good time. Drive careful."

I would say, "Okay. Bye. I'll be back by 1:00 a.m. Don't wait up."

One day that fall, I called Jim Eckhart, one of my poker friends. I knew he probably had a spare bedroom at his house. I said, "Jim, this is Bill."

"How's it going?" Jim asked.

"Well, not so good," I said.

"What's wrong?"

"Do you guys have a spare bedroom at your house?"

"Yeah. Why?"

"Ask your parents if I can live there."

"Why, are things tough at home?"

"Well, I have a girlfriend now. Her name is Angie, and my dad doesn't like it when I go out with her."

"Why not?"

"I think he's jealous because he wants me to stick around here with him."

"Is your mom—" he said, pausing before I interrupted.

"My mom, I guess, is the root of the problem. She can't talk normally, which I guess is why my dad wants me to stay home and keep him company. He's lonely."

"I see," he said. "Well, I'll ask my parents."

I said, "It's not for sure yet. I have to see how things go."

"Okay, I'll be talking to you."

"Okay. Thanks. Bye."

After a while I decided that for leaving home to really be worth it, Angie and I would have to have been really getting along. At the time, I figured that it was good to put up with my dad because then he would pay for college. If I had left home before graduation, he might not have paid for college. I mistakenly thought college was essential. In reality there are a lot of good jobs that do not require a degree.

The stress of my dad's yelling really only lasted about an hour into my dates with Angie. It took about twenty minutes to drive to her house. I was very much looking forward to seeing Angie, but I was still thinking about my dad's yelling.

We often walked around a lake.

A few times I said, "My dad doesn't like it when we go out."

We were getting along very poorly, so all she said was, "Oh."

We were both very inexperienced in romance, which hurt our relationship a lot.

I paused and waited for her to say more. She didn't.

I said, "I think it's because he's jealous because he wants me to stay home with him. My mom had a stroke and she can't talk normally, so I think he's lonely."

"Oh, that's too bad," said Angie.

I just hugged her and said, "Well, I'll ignore him."

I often wished I could live with her family. Yet we were never getting along well enough for me to mention that even as a fantasy. It just wasn't done that much anyway. I was seventeen, and she was sixteen.

I tried to get her to talk about anything, to act bubbly. She never really did. We talked about our classes sometimes. Just being with her was pleasant, though, even if we didn't talk much. However, she often seemed a little upset with me. We went to movies and a couple of Shakespearean plays, but we were lousy communicators. About all she talked about some nights was the plot of the Shakespeare play we were about to see, so that I would understand the play. Still, I felt it was better to have a quiet girlfriend than no girlfriend at all.

It was her being annoyed that also caused me to compromise with myself. I figured that seeing her only once a week was enough. If she was annoyed on Saturday night, I didn't want to call her back until Tuesday. Then we made plans for the next weekend. It seemed necessary to give her several days' notice. She always agreed to go out with me the next weekend, but there was always some doubt in my mind whether she would agree or not. However, through September and October of 1976, I was still optimistic. I felt things with Angie would eventually work out.

By rationalizing that I really had to do homework on weekday nights, and by rationalizing that I really had to see my male poker friends once a week, I decided that it was reasonable to see Angie only once a week.

In spite of the fact that we had an imperfect relationship, this period was actually the happiest time in my life, ever. Angie still was more of a plus than a minus. I was so happy that when I woke up a couple minutes before my alarm rang every morning, I lay there hoping for it to ring! I was looking forward to each new day that much. I was going to school six-and-a-half hours per day and was enjoying it. I was working out for swimming three hours a day and enjoying that. I was studying three hours a day. Life was really very fun. I was happy with myself. I had pride in everything I was doing. Each day was a new adventure and a chance to achieve something new, fun, and positive. I liked doing well on tests in school.

As my relationship with Angie grew worse, I started going to some parties held by people from my school. I was hoping to run into Melanie Carson. I never did. She was the rock singer who had sat beside me in physics class. I still considered her one of the most desirable girls in the school. She was never in any of my classes again.

At the beginning of November, something awful happened. Someone stole my letter jacket. I left it hanging up in my unlocked locker in the general locker room. The season hadn't started yet, so I didn't have a varsity locker. I was depressed for a week. The letter jackets take about six weeks to order, and by then it would've been winter, when it is too wet to wear one. I reported the theft to the police, but they weren't able to do anything. I was depressed about the loss of the jacket for about five days. I had never felt that bad for five days in a row in my life. Then, I cheered up a bit.

For the next couple of weeks, my mood was a little down. I didn't call Angie, and she didn't call me.

Swim practice started then, and I was about the fastest on our team in every event except backstroke, but I didn't feel as happy about it as I had expected.

After not seeing Angie for a few weeks, I became what I thought was indifferent about her. I was a little down in mood and was thinking maybe I'd be happier dating someone else. I called her and said, "I'm sorry I haven't called you for so long."

Hesitantly, she said, "That's … okay," with a strained voice.

I said, "I don't know how to tell you this, but let's go out with other people." She started crying, and I said, "Is everything else okay?"

She said tearfully, "Yeah."

I said, "I'm sorry. You can still call me sometime."

She never did.

That was the start of my chronic manic depression.

I was still looking forward somewhat to a good swimming season. In December, we had our first meet. I went 1:13.5 in the 100-yard breaststroke and did some equivalent time in the fifty-yard breaststroke in the medley relay. I was very disappointed with my breaststroke times. I had averaged 1:13.5 the previous year. I had gone 1:13 point something in our fifteen meets, except for the first one and the last two during the previous season. I thought all my work in the off-season should have made me go 1:09.5.

The first major casualty of the depressed phase would be my swimming. At the time, it felt like my poor swimming caused my depression, but in hindsight it seems likely that my depression caused my poor swimming. There was somewhat of a vicious circle. This is because once manic depression starts by a triggering event, it goes on, and on, and on, indefinitely. Then the disease causes sad events. Sad events don't cause the disease. Depression interferes with concentration and therefore interferes with athletic ability. You lose competitions, and that is sad. It interferes with concentration, and therefore you lose work and school ability. It is depressing to do a bad job at work or school because of poor concentration. A chronic depression that goes on and on causes irritability, which makes you lose friends. Depression can cause suicide, and then you lose everything.

The most stressful event triggering the disease was my break-up with Angie. I got the genes for susceptibility to manic depression from my mom. If I would have had a successful, romantic, continuing relationship with Angie, my manic depression may have been delayed indefinitely. I could have avoided the stress of breaking up. On the other hand, having a steady relationship is not the treatment or prevention for manic depression. Relationships can be stressful. Happily married people can get manic depression. Single manic-depressives can get married and it certainly doesn't cure them. Also, breaking up is depressing for everyone. However, most people cheer up in a few weeks after a break-up.

Fortunately for humanity, only 0.5 percent of the population comes down with type-one manic depression. Type-ones lose touch with reality when they get manic. We get grandiose delusions and paranoid delusions, which are ridiculous ideas or reactions from normal sights and sounds. This is different from hallucinations, which are sights and sounds that are not really there. The 0.5 per cent of the population that gets type-one manic depression has the genes for it. Another smaller fraction of a percent of the population have the genes for it but are lucky enough to go their whole lives without the disease. Type-two manic depressives do not get delusional, but they do get some of the other symptoms of mania, so it is sometimes a problem. Both types get badly depressed at times.

The classic example of someone with type-two manic depression is British Prime Minister Winston Churchill. During World War II in the 1940s, he had enough manic energy to stay up late and give speeches that inspired his nation to save the world from destruction by the Nazi Germans. If he had had type one, like me, he would've been in the hospital for months or years at a time. He would not have been Prime Minister.

Manic depression is also called bipolar affective disorder. Bipolar means having two extremes. Affective means having to do with mood. One extreme of mood is depression, which is a period when there is prolonged sadness, crying, low self-esteem, suicidal thoughts or actions, and many more symptoms. The other extreme of mood, a manic episode, was described in the first chapter, KGB Bloodhounds. This is when you feel so great about yourself that you think you are an FBI agent, God, Jesus, the President, or the musician John Lennon, for example. You are laughing, you are happy, you don't sleep, and you are totally out of touch with reality.

A full 15 percent of the population does get depressive illness. This is also called unipolar affective disorder. These people have problems with depression but never get manic.

A complete list of symptoms of depression and mania can be found at the end of this book. I inherited the genes for type-one manic depression from my mother. If I had an identical twin, he'd have a 70 percent chance of getting it some time in his life. If I were to have children, roughly one out of seven of my children would get the disease. The genes just make you susceptible to it. It usually takes environmental stress to trigger it. Once manic depression starts, though, it has a life of its own. When my manic depression started, the biochemical agents in my brain were present in the wrong amounts. My mind's neurotransmitters—such as norepinephrine, serotonin, dopamine, and others known or still unidentified—were malfunctioning. There are medications that help a lot in restoring the chemical balance, but they are not perfect. Still, medication is the hero of this book.

CHAPTER 5

DEPRESSION SLOWS MY SWIMMING

We had a meet that Friday, December 17, which was right before the start of Christmas vacation. We were competing against Kent. They had an outstanding team, but we knew we could keep it close if we swam well. Anyway, I went 1:15.3 in the 100-yard breaststroke. That was a terrible time. I didn't know what was wrong with me. I would learn much later that what was wrong with me was depression.

The next night was the Winter Fling Dance held by our school. It was a girl-ask-guy dance. A girl named Emily asked me to the dance. We went on the date, but I was feeling so awful that I was silently narrating to myself the story of this date, and the story seemed to be a tragedy. The narrator was a cross between horror science fiction narrator Rod Serling and sportscaster Howard Cosell. It was the tragic story of a date that was supposed to be fun but instead was not. My internal narration went like this:

Here is the tragic story of a man who was a potential star athlete. He recently swam the unspeakable time of 1:15.3, and can never redo that race. He should be noticing how fancy everyone's clothes are; instead, he dwells on the fact that his date, Emily, needs a tan. He forgets it's December. He should think, *What a nice, cross-cultural, educational, and adventurous experience it is to eat at a foreign restaurant.* He should be enjoying it. Instead, he is thinking, *This food is foreign, so it won't be any good.* He should be feeling very sophisticated, stylish, and grown up, and should be doing his best to make sure his date has fun. Instead he wants to go home and cry. He wants to go sit in his bedroom and regroup, retrench, retreat, or redirect. He wants to figure out how he has managed to enter *The Twilight Zone.*

I thought, *How could I have a good time when I swam so slow?* I think I remember wishing Emily would ask me about my classes because I was still doing well at those. Also, I could've told her about my parents if she would have asked. However, I was too quiet to bring either of these topics up. I was too busy bumming out. At the end of the date when she asked me in, I declined and just gave her a quick kiss goodnight. I didn't want to pretend to be having a good time anymore.

I drove home thinking, *This is now the tragic story of a romance that could've happened if things were normal, but they were not.*

Over winter vacation, I participated in winter vacation swim practice. Each practice session was up to three hours long and was supposed to be some of the hardest and most beneficial all year. I had lost my ability to push myself in practice. Now everyone was beating me at every stroke. Even a new swimmer was beating me. I was falling apart, and I didn't know why. I should have been swimming faster.

I also knew I was supposed to be having more fun at the two parties I went to that vacation. One was a party put on by one of the CITs from the previous summer. Most of the CITs were at the party. I remember watching a few people play Nerf basketball. They were definitely having fun. I was very envious. I remember thinking that everyone else at the party knew how to have fun except me. I again narrated to myself: Here were normal people having fun, and I was not normal. I had the same thought at a New Year's Eve party, thrown by a classmate who I didn't know that well. I had the thought that I was not having a normal good time. In spite of this pessimistic outlook, I *did* get some New Year's kisses, including one from Melanie Carson whom I liked so much. That was the high point of the evening.

We had a meet coming up against our neighborhood rival, an all-boys Catholic prep school, St. John's. A fellow student asked me if we were going to win.

I said, "I'm winning my event." Little did he know that as I sat there, I was narrating my life story in my mind, and the story was again a tragedy. It was the story of a star falling apart, never to be heard from again.

I was getting more and more depressed, and my schoolwork started to suffer. My swimming suffered also. In the meet against St. John's, I swam 1:16.2 in the 100-yard breaststroke. That was a terrible time. I came in last place. We lost the meet by one point. If I would've just gone 1:15.9, we would've won.

Later that night, I went to a poker game, and my friend Jack Johnson said, "How's it going?"

I said, "Pretty good."

Jack said, "That's good."

I said, "Well, actually not good."

"What's wrong?"

"I need a new family."

"Play cards," said Ed Lundbland.

We just left it at that. Getting away from my dad would have been nice, but now I had an illness, and I didn't know it. My poker friends, swim teammates, and family didn't know it. I inaccurately blamed my dad. The main problem was the genes I got from my mom. I didn't know that. The thought of going to a psychiatrist occurred to me, but I didn't see how it could help.

In swim practice, I should have been concentrating on making my muscles hurt as much as I could stand, while trying hard to catch the guy ahead of me. Instead I was obsessed as follows:

I am nobody. Here I am swimming behind Jack the sophomore and Kurt the senior rookie, and they are beating me. I'm a nobody. I'm supposed to be the senior expert. I am nobody. I lead off in the lane and they catch me, or sometimes they loaf and don't catch me because they are goof-offs, but they beat me in meets anyway. I am nobody. Come on, pull-exhale, pull-exhale. What type of boyfriend am I to bring home to Daddy when I'm such a nobody that I sacrifice all summer and fall just to end up swimming slow? Jack has such big feet. Try to catch them. I'm a nobody. It was such a gamble to swim that much last summer for the winter varsity season pay-off. Now I'm still slower than the average putz. This pool is crowded. We need wider lanes. Darn cheap school. I'm a nobody. I am a nobody because I still lose to Jack and Kurt in meets. Jack has big feet. C'mon pull-exhale, pull-exhale. I need to win districts to redeem myself. Too bad I'm rated so far down the list. I am a nobody. Here comes a wall. Do a turn, duh … I turn like a peon. Why can't I have a normal happy high school experience? Instead I'm in this dark quagmire far from earth. This is the pits. I am no one.

Thoughts like those would repeat continuously through swim practice and more and more through much of the day.

There was a bright spot to that January. The list of people going on the senior class trip to Jamaica came out. Luckily, my dad let me go and paid for it. There were about twenty-five girls and twenty-five guys going. I looked at the list and was pleased to find out that Melanie Carson was going.

A bunch of other cool people were going, so it seemed like it would be a fun trip. It would be a great vacation.

Meanwhile, the swimming season was going ahead as scheduled for most of the team. I continued to do lousy and was getting more and more depressed. Jack and Kurt were both beating me in breaststroke. This was especially embarrassing because Kurt had not swum since eighth grade, and he was now a senior. Also, Jack was a sophomore.

I even called our last year's captain out of retirement to watch my turns and stroke. He said, "The problem is all in your head." I didn't know exactly what he meant, except that maybe I needed a shrink. He was right, as it turns out; I did need a shrink.

I was becoming much less smooth in other areas. At card games, Stan would get upset with me after I didn't show my cards when I had bluffed or just plain bet him out of a hand. The best strategy is not to show your hand when you don't have to. It is nicer and friendlier to show your cards, though. I felt that because I was losing so badly in swimming, I had to make it up in cards, so I wouldn't show, and he would wonder out loud why I was invited to the games. My selfishness could be put under the general category of the irritability symptom of depression.

The situation usually went something like this. Stan said, "If I drop, are you going to show?"

I said, "Maybe. Don't drop."

Stan said, "C'mon it's a friendly game."

Jim said, "It's nicer to show."

I said, "It's bad strategy."

"Just show. I drop," he said, dropping his hand face down.

Then, shoving my hand under some other cards, I said, "For another quarter you could have seen them. It's bad strategy to show." Then I pulled in the pile of money.

Stan said, "I don't know why we even invite this asshole. It's a friendly game."

I couldn't see the value of being friendlier. I felt that because I was losing in swimming, I had to be sure to win at cards. It is really too bad because Stan and I had been friends for five years at that point and had rarely had an argument. Our friendship survived these games, but the arguments certainly didn't help.

My grades were falling, too. Poor concentration is a symptom of depression. Usually it's because one is so preoccupied with some worry. In my case, it was swimming.

The regional meet was the last chance of my life to make all my hard swimming work pay off. It was also a chance for me to improve my mood. I felt like crying as I got on the starting block. I swam a time of 1:13.9, last in my heat. Then I went in the shower and cried. With the shower pouring on my face, nobody could see that I was crying. This was more crying than the average defeated athlete should do. This was the depressed part of manic depression. I stayed in the shower about ten minutes. Then I went back to where our team was sitting, and I tried to give away my swim cap and goggles. I didn't deserve to own them. Maybe one of the juniors could make them go faster next year than I managed to make them go this year. My teammates just ignored me. Nobody would take them. They didn't know what to say.

One of the juniors sat next to me and said, "No, keep your cap and goggles. You didn't do that bad."

I kept saying to him, "How could I get slower than last year? How could I get slower?"

"I don't know. That happens a lot. You weren't that much slower," he said.

"I was a lot slower. I swam 1:10 last year. Watch this heat."

We watched another heat of the breaststroke preliminaries. We saw times of 1:08 through 1:12.

I said to him, "I could have beat half those guys last year. With some modest improvement, I could have won that heat."

He said something like, "Don't worry about it. You did okay."

Talking to him helped cheer me up a bit. That was nice.

I went to a couple of swim practices that next week. The practices were to help the team prepare for the state meet, which I had not qualified for. I stayed in my clothes, though. I sat on the bench on the side of the pool. It felt better to be there than to be at home. At home, I would have had for company my mother, one or two of my little brothers, and one of our paid household helpers. I preferred the team. When I was home, I had begun to sit in my room alone and obsess to myself. I would go over the same "I'm a nobody" thoughts outlined before, but it was now much worse. After the state meet, swimming was over. There was about a month before the trip to Jamaica. I was badly depressed that whole month.

We were scheduled to leave for the trip to Jamaica on April 2. I was incredibly depressed until the trip. In school, I couldn't pay attention. It was lucky for me that last semester grades didn't count for class rank. When I got home from school, I just sat in my room and obsessed to myself. I went over and over the swimming season in my mind. I was obsessed with how badly I swam. I didn't do any homework until I had agonized to myself about swimming for about two hours. I started falling way behind in school. In the fall, I had planned on doing well in school in the spring because swimming would be over. I should have had more time to do homework. I hadn't planned on being devastated.

In the meantime, before the trip, I felt I couldn't justify my existence. I had swum so much and gained so little. I figured I had wasted a lot of time swimming, just proving that I was in no way an athlete. I thought, this is when some people commit suicide, but I would never do that. That would really be admitting defeat. I thought I would gradually recover in a few weeks, but I was wrong.

Chapter 6

Melanie Carson

In the airport gate area while we were waiting for our flight to Jamaica, I tried to get Melanie's attention, but she ignored me. It didn't matter that much, because I had a whole week to get her attention.

The plane ride was fairly uneventful.

Our luggage was sent automatically to our hotel. We just had to get on our bus to Montego Bay and go to our hotel. We checked out our hotel rooms. Some of our friends were right above us. We saw them on their balcony when we were on ours. We were on the fourth floor, and they were on the fifth.

Just for the fun of it, I said, "Hey, we can climb up to your room from ours." I just stood on the rail, but one of my roommates climbed all the way up.

The next thing we knew, there were cops pulling guns on us. Somebody had thought we were burglars when they saw us climbing the balcony. We explained that these were our rooms and we were just having fun.

The cops finally said, "Okay, no problem."

After that, we headed down to the bar for a beer. We (my roommates and about four others) all ordered a beer. The talk turned to how to maintain a supply of beer for the week. There was a liquor store across the street from our hotel.

One guy said, "If we each buy a case on one day, we can share and all have some beer."

I said, "I'm not in on that. I'm not going to drink that much."

He said, "Okay."

I finished my beer and said, "I'm going to take off. I might be back in awhile."

I went to look for Melanie and her roommates—Paula, Pattie, and Katie. I found them right in the lobby outside the bar. I said, "Do you guys want to take a walk on the beach?"

They agreed, and so we went for a walk. I figured being with four girls was a special treat. Still, because I was depressed, it wasn't quite as fun as I knew it was supposed to be. We walked for a way, and then we took off our shoes and socks and rolled up our pants legs and ran. It was fun.

Paula was the leader. On the way back from the beach, she walked ahead of us a bit, so once—at my suggestion—we hid in some trees to make it look like we ditched her. She saw us and quit walking so far ahead. I tried to talk to Melanie but had better luck talking to Katie. Melanie and Katie were close friends, so I wanted Katie to like me, too.

When we got to the front steps of our hotel, some of our group was standing on the steps. One of the guys looked surprised when he saw me with all those girls, especially Katie with whom he apparently was good friends. Katie and he said something to each other, which let me know they were good friends. I went up to my room.

In my room was a bunch of guys. They asked where I had been, and I told them I had gone for a walk with Melanie, Pattie, Paula, and Katie. They seemed a little surprised but hid it pretty well. We hung around and talked for a while.

That night, we went to sleep at a reasonable hour. We had been up since very early that morning, and we had to be on the tour bus at 8:00 a.m.

The next morning, we got up, grabbed some breakfast, and went over to Ocho Rios for Dunn's River Falls. They were beautiful, and we waded in them. I had on a suntan lotion that was supposed to have extra sunburn protection. That was before the sun protection factor numbers came out, but I know now its strength was the equivalent of SPF 6. It was a cloudy day, but our teachers who were leading the group had warned us that you can get burned even on a cloudy day. We stayed until noon, and then we headed back to Montego Bay.

Later, I lay out in the sun with my roommate and swim teammate, Jeff. I still had the number 6 lotion on. It was still cloudy. That night it was clear that I hadn't gotten much sun.

Later, a bunch of us had a beer and a "compare your sunburn" party in one of our school's hotel rooms.

For the first few days of this trip, I continued to talk to Melanie and Katie whenever I could find the chance.

The next morning, we took a tour of a haunted mansion and then headed for the beach. It was cloudy again, but since I had been repeatedly warned that you can get burned even on a cloudy day, I put on the number 6 lotion and lay out for an hour on each side.

Again, that night, I had no color. Some people were starting to get tan, and I was envious.

The next day, I went for it. It was sunny, and I lay out for an hour and a half on each side with no lotion and no shirt. I got very sunburned. It took about three hours before it hit me; then I started to feel like I was going to faint. Then I got the chills and started shivering. My roommates laughed at first, but then they got concerned. I was too embarrassed and depressed to tell them to call an ambulance, but I needed one. I decided to treat myself. That was stupid. I decided that the chills were from shock, so I thought I needed to keep warm, so I took a hot bath. Years later, I was told that you get the chills when your body temperature is rising even though that doesn't make sense. When you are burned, your skin can't breathe and you overheat. A cold bath would've been right, but instead I took a hot bath. My body temperature was probably 105 degrees. I could have died.

How could such a smart guy have been so stupid? Simple. Depressed people are accident-prone. When depressed, you can be so preoccupied with one worry that you neglect all else. In this case, it was my obsession with how poorly I swam.

It was about dinnertime when I went into the tub. One roommate checked on me, and I said I felt okay. Then they went out on the town, dancing and drinking. I got out of the tub after awhile and just lay on a bed. I stayed in bed until dinner the next day. The morning of the next day, one of our teachers who was chaperoning us checked on me, and I said I was all right—just weak and sore.

The day after that, I went back on the tour, wearing long pants and sunblock on my arms. I got some sympathy from Katie and Melanie, which was nice. Katie said, "Does it hurt?"

I said, "It only hurts when I breathe."

Melanie said, "Well, just don't breathe then."

Katie said, "When do you think you'll be able to go out in the sun again?"

"September."

One evening we saw a nightclub act that included an Elvis impersonator who was pretty good. Melanie went, but I didn't manage to talk to her much.

One day, a bunch of guys were sitting by themselves, each in his own seat on the tour bus. Melanie walked onto the bus and said, "Who wants the privilege of sitting with me?"

I hesitated and said, "I do."

We talked about the tourist sight we had just seen. Having her next to me was a thrill. Now I remember really debating whether or not to hold her hand.

I thought, *Should I hold her hand for just a second and then let go? Should I say anything about holding her hand while I'm holding it?* Everyone was watching. *Does that matter?* I wondered.

Just sitting next to her was pleasant. I figured there would be plenty of time for holding hands later. I just tried to keep up friendly conversation.

The next day was kind of cloudy, so another guy and I rented mopeds and went riding up in the hills. There was very beautiful natural scenery with lots of tropical vegetation.

The last night, I went looking for Melanie at her room. She wasn't there. Eventually I found her in the bar of our hotel, talking to another girl from our school. They were talking about class rank or something and how you could take easier classes and get an A and get higher class rank. I sat down and listened, and then the girl asked me where all the really smart kids were going to college—like Barry and Eugene.

I said, "Barry is going to USC, and Eugene is going to the University of Washington."

"Where are you going?" she asked.

"Well, I don't know yet," I said. "I applied to Stanford, Yale, the University of Puget Sound, and the University of Washington. Stanford and Yale are hard to get into. You have to have very good grades and test scores."

"Well, you'll get into the University of Washington," said Melanie.

I said, "Yeah, but I'm worried about getting rejected from Stanford and Yale." (I had also applied to Harvard, but had given up on it.)

"What did you get on your SATs?" the other girl asked.

"Well, the first time I took it, I didn't do so hot, so then I took it again and got 690 verbal, 740 math," I said.

"What percentile is that?"

"Ninety-ninth."

Melanie said, "Well, I think you've got nothing to worry about."

The other girl said, "So do I."

I could tell by the look on Melanie's face that she was impressed.

The singer from the band was calling everybody up to dance, so I asked Melanie to dance. We did one slow dance, but I remember thinking it didn't feel as good as it should. I thought, *If only my father approved of dating like other fathers. Maybe then it would feel good.* Actually, I needed to not be depressed; then it would have felt good, regardless of my dad.

There were three couples from our school dancing including us, so after the first dance I said, "Rotate."

We changed partners. I don't know what I was thinking.

The next day, on the plane on the way home, I felt on the one hand that my sunburn was a disaster, but on the other hand, at least I could ask Melanie out when we got home.

That first week after the Jamaica trip, the whole school knew about my sunburn. I got some sympathy and some teasing. I was depressed but not too badly. Also, that week, I got rejection letters from Harvard, Stanford, and Yale.

I had gotten accepted by the University of Puget Sound in Tacoma, and I had already been accepted by UW Seattle. I would go to Puget Sound in Tacoma, to get away from home.

The very good news that week was that Melanie agreed to go out with me. We planned to see the movie *Rocky* on Friday.

I told my dad I was going out with Melanie.

My dad asked, "Where do you know her from?"

"School."

"Is she Jewish?"

"No."

"What are you going out with a girl who's not Jewish for?" he asked.

This was the first time in his life he had indicated to me that Judaism was important. At first I thought he was just implying that he thought that *I* thought it was important. When I was younger, my mother and father had both clearly said that it was okay to marry a non-Jew.

I said, "I'm going out with her because I like her."

I got up and carried my dishes to the sink.

He got up from his chair, followed me, and yelled, "Just a minute. I don't like the idea of you going out with a girl who isn't Jewish!"

"Why don't you like it?" I asked, annoyed.

"I don't think it's *good* to go out with someone who is *not Jewish!*" he said angrily, standing near me.

I walked away and he followed me and I asked, "What's not good about it?"

My dad yelled, "You shouldn't go *out* with someone who *isn't Jewish!*"

"What about that Newman or that Stein girl you used to go out with?" he asked, naming two girls, each of whom I had gone out with only once.

I said, "I'm going out with Melanie now."

He yelled, "I don't *like* that idea!"

"Why not?"

"I don't know if I *approve* of that!"

My mood lowered drastically. I went back to my room and finished getting ready. I had hoped going out with Melanie would cheer me up because I was really looking forward to it. Now it was leading to more problems. I looked at the situation pessimistically, being depressed. I thought that this would end up like Romeo and Juliet—in other words, a romantic tragedy—if I didn't play my cards right. I thought that now things were going to be really difficult. We would have to elope or just plain run away. How would I explain to my friends that I had been banished from my family? Or that I had dumped my family? I couldn't tell exactly what it would be. It was supposed to be just a date between two high school students. They sing about this all the time on the radio in Beach Boys songs and Beatles songs. Why couldn't it be like that? My friends did not fully understand the situation in my house. Even I didn't know that things would get this bad. My dad had been nice for a month or so, and then he suddenly attacked. Even in the fall when I was dating Angie, he was nice six out of seven days of the week. He only screamed on days I saw her.

This was my state of mind as I left and drove over to Melanie's house. While I was driving, I began to feel somewhat better. Even though we'd be going to different colleges, I thought, we could still see each other on vacations. I thought that maybe I could tell Melanie that my dad had gotten mad but that I'd just ignore him. As I got near her house, though, I started narrating the story of this date in my mind: the tragic story of how the date *would* go, compared to how it *should* go, how I was supposed to be happy and proud to introduce myself to her parents, instead of feeling embarrassed that I was a Jew who couldn't swim well. My swimming failure had not been on my mind that day until after my dad yelled at me.

When I got to her door, her mother answered, and all I said was, "Hi."

Melanie came to the door, and as we left her mother said, "Have a good time." I was so pessimistic about parents that I thought she was being sarcastic. I really thought her mother was being sarcastic.

Melanie and I walked up to my car.

In a cheerful voice, she said, "Is this your car?"

"Um, ah, it's my mom's."

"She lets you use it?"

"Uh, yeah."

I opened the door for her, but then I couldn't figure out if I was supposed to shut it or if she was. It was awfully poor form—not at all smooth. Finally, she shut the door.

I walked around the front of the car to my side and got in.

I kept thinking of what I *would* be saying if only I felt normal. Things like, "You look nice. I'm so glad we're together." Instead, I said hardly anything, at first.

I asked her where she was going to go to college. She said, "Pacific Lutheran University (PLU)."

I asked, "Where is that?"

She said, "Tacoma."

I was going to go to UPS, also in Tacoma. I *should've been overjoyed* that we would be going to school in the same town. Instead, because I had already obsessed about Tacoma being the pits, I came up with a new pessimistic thought. I thought, *Oh no. We'll be going to rival schools.*

So, I just said, "Oh, I'm going to the University of Puget Sound, also in Tacoma."

Then I asked, "Why are you going there?" My mood was so low that I think I even sounded argumentative because I had never heard of it, like I had heard of Stanford.

She said, "It's a family tradition. My parents and my brothers went there."

I said, "I'm not looking forward to graduation, because high school was fun, and college just won't be the same."

The whole date went badly. I was distant, negative, and grumpy, and unable to tell her why. It is hard to break up on the first date. I had most recently been depressed about swimming. My depressive obsessive thoughts switched from my dad and went back to swimming. You cannot choose your obsession or switch it off. I went on and on about how poorly I had done in swimming.

I remember saying, "Now if you practice and practice at something, you are supposed to get better at it, aren't you? Well, don't you think so? I got worse at it!"

Melanie just sat there, kind of speechless. My voice was so irritated that it probably sounded like I was upset with her.

I kept on going. I said, "You know I swam the 100-yard breast stroke. My times actually got slower. I actually got slower and slower. Can you believe it? I was supposed to get faster, right?"

Melanie continued to sit there in stunned silence.

I continued. "Well, I got slower," I said. "I actually got slower, and it is bumming me out."

In Jamaica, I had been much calmer than this. I was never very visibly upset about anything. Not even the sunburn had upset me this much.

I forgot the rule that you're supposed to impress your date, instead of dwell on your bad points. What could be simpler? However, in my state of mind, nothing was simple.

I never even told her about my dad's opposition to our dating. I was paralyzed with depression. When I thought about my dad for a second, I felt like crying, so I avoided the topic. Crying is not a great dating strategy.

We saw the movie and it was all right. When Rocky ate raw eggs, Melanie said, "Maybe you should have done that for swimming."

I knew she was trying to help me feel better, but I felt bad that it was not enough.

We came out, and I held her hand as we walked to the car.

When I held her hand it felt like she was a really close friend.

She asked, "What do you want to do now?"

The words "make out" came to mind, but I said, "I don't know. Let's just drive around."

We drove around a lot, talking. I did not say anything impressive or express any enthusiasm. Finally, we stopped at a McDonald's, and I got up the guts to tell her I had heard her class rank was 26 out of 543. We talked about that for a few minutes, but I never got to the point of saying how impressed I was with her or that I thought we had something in common, academic ability, or that we should see a lot of each other.

My brain had only been malfunctioning for a couple of months, and on the one hand I thought I would recover. On the other hand, that night I was so depressed I couldn't bring myself to say anything positive about myself. I just said stuff like, "College just isn't going to be the same. I'll miss my friends."

She asked me a bunch of questions in a friendly way to try to get to a topic that would be easy, pleasant, or relevant. She was very nice.

I drove her home and tried to walk her to the door, but she kept saying, "Good night, good night." Then she went inside without letting me kiss her.

I was so frustrated that I drove around aimlessly for half an hour. I didn't know what to do. There was a card game that night, but if I had gone there, my friends would have asked a lot of questions about the date. So, I just went home.

The next few days, I was really frustrated and baffled. I got up enough nerve to ask Melanie to the senior prom, but she said, "I don't think so."

I was really disappointed. So I asked Donna Freeman, a longtime friend.

She accepted.

I went to prom with Donna and a couple of my poker friends and their dates. It was fairly uneventful, but I kept wishing I was there with Melanie.

Graduation day came. I graduated with distinction, but I was depressed that I was leaving high school without a girlfriend. That thought ruined graduation for me.

CHAPTER 7

HOTEL CALIFORNIA ISRAEL

Summer began, and I had three weeks to kill. I had been rehired to be a camp counselor at Camp Okransky, but I knew I was in no shape to handle it, so I opted for six weeks in Israel on a tour with the JTG Israel Pilgrimage. Being a tourist is usually easier than working on a job.

I looked forward to possibly finding a girl to date on the tour of Israel, a Jewish nation.

During World War II, the German Nazis killed six million Jews in the Holocaust. Unfortunately, since then, some Jews have felt that most non-Jews are potential Nazis. Some Jews are prejudiced against non-Jews. They feel that Jews are morally and intellectually superior.

So, I felt I could not really discuss Melanie with some of my friends, who happened to be Jewish, because Melanie was a "goy." Goy is a derogatory word for non-Jew.

Some of my friends might have said, "Why do you like a goy?"

Many of my friends' parents were sincere when they said, "You should marry a Jew."

My parents were less religious, and in normal times of my family, before my mom had her stroke, both of my parents made it clear that they would not mind at all if I married a non-Jew. They would have trusted my own judgment for whom to marry.

Being so depressed and preoccupied, I wasn't really looking forward to going to Israel, although logically I should have been. Unfortunately, with manic depressive illness, logic does not play a part. Instead, a depressed person looks at the worst side of all situations.

I had been told to read a book about Israeli Prime Minister Golda Meir in preparation for the trip. I remember lying out in the sun on my stomach. My sunburn had healed. I was trying to read the book about Golda Meir, but I couldn't concentrate. I remember wondering what could be wrong with my brain. It was horrifying. Still, I thought I would gradually cheer up.

On Thursday, June 23, I started to switch to a manic phase. I had a poker game that evening at my house, and with some luck, I won a lot of money. I remember thinking I could tell what cards people had by reading their faces. A little bit of face reading is normal, but I started to think I could do it extraordinarily well. We played poker until 3:30 a.m., so I didn't get to bed until 4:00 a.m.

Friday evening, I tried to do the dishes, but I was lost in thought. I thought of all the people I knew and their different relationships. It took me four hours to do the dishes for six people, and we had a dishwasher.

My dad came into the kitchen at about ten thirty that night and said, "Bill, what's wrong? Are you lost in thought?"

I said, "Well, yes. I'm just thinking about the people I know and our family. Mom's not going to get any better, is she?"

"Well, no," he said. "It's really doubtful."

This is something that I already had known for a long time, but now I was thinking about it more in depth. I finished the dishes and went to bed. That night I didn't sleep. I just lay in bed thinking and thinking about different people in my life and what they had in their lives that I did not. I also tried to figure out what made them happier and what made their lives go so much more smoothly than mine. Finally, at about five thirty in the morning, it really struck me that my mother couldn't talk to me. I cried myself to sleep. Being manic is usually like being in a good mood that involves no crying, but when manic, you can switch back and forth between being manic and being depressed. The inability to sleep was a sign of mania.

At about eight in the morning, my whole family got up because we were going to a mountain park for an overnight camping trip.

At the breakfast table, I told the whole family, "You know, Mom's stroke just hit me last night. When it first happened, we were in Florida, and Dad called us from the hospital and he was crying on the phone. Then Steve, you started crying, and Rick you started crying, and Johnny was too young to know what was going on. So, I took the phone from Steve, and got the information on where the tickets were, what to do for a cab, and packed our suitcases so we could fly home that day as scheduled because we had to be back for school. Then we got home to Seattle, and Mom and Dad were still in Florida. Having no parents around was kind of fun. Mom was in the hospital in Florida, and Dad stayed with her, but I figured she'd get better. I didn't worry. I wanted to go to swim practice. When Mom and Dad got home, I saw how Mom was, and I didn't want her to live like that, but I thought, *In the meantime she can't yell at me.* Mom and I had argued a lot up to that point. Now I realize it's a big problem to have your Mom be unable to talk to you."

My older brother, Steve, said, "I thought it was good that you took responsibility for the tickets and kept your act together. I felt bad for you that you couldn't feel bad with us."

I said, "Well it's not good to feel bad, but I feel bad now. I didn't sleep last night until 5:30 a.m. when I cried myself to sleep. I guess my feelings on this are just coming out now." (This idea—that strong feelings or anger coming out long after the incident that caused them is a cause of mental illness—was something I had heard of at that point, so I said it. Now I believe it is a myth.)

Steve said something like, "It's good that you're thinking about it now."

That was the end of the discussion for then. We went up to the mountains. That day, Jack Johnson, one of my poker friends, was having a graduation party at a different spot that was not too far from ours. I was already in a fog. I was switching back and forth from being depressed to being manic. I drove separately.

In the car on the way over to Jack's party, I was crying so hard I couldn't see to drive sometimes. I was crying because I knew the situation in my home would not get any better. My dad would always be jealous of my girlfriends, and my mom would not recover. My mom should be a dear, sweet, capable, warm, friendly, communicative, ambitious mother. Instead, she couldn't talk to me. She could hardly walk, and she couldn't read or write. She could hardly do anything. She used to help guide my life and actually did a good job. She could watch over me and be glad if I had a girlfriend. Now she could not do anything like this, like the other mothers I knew. (She was also depressed to begin with, as a result of her own manic depression. I didn't know this at the time.) Thinking about the effects of my mom's stroke made me cry so hard that I had to pull the car over because the tears interfered with my vision.

When I pulled up at Jack's party, it occurred to me to tell Mr. and Mrs. Johnson what I was going through to see if they could help. Then I thought, *No, this is a party. It would ruin the party.*

As I got out of the car, I apparently switched back to the manic phase because I quit crying. I joined the party. There was a volleyball game going on. I did well in it because volleyballs are like tetherballs, and I had played tetherball in my backyard since I was five. I was also experiencing the manic energy and hyperactivity that made this volleyball game feel extra good. I had decided that a good mental attitude could help one do anything well. In a way, this is very true. During the volleyball game, I had a good attitude. Or, at least I felt good. I may have seemed too hyper. When we weren't playing, I felt worse, though. It felt good when a girl put some suntan lotion on my face.

The rest of the party went okay for me until the end. As I was leaving and fearing a cry coming on again, I turned to one of my friends and said, "I'm crashing."

He said, "Oh you'll have a good time in Israel. I know it."

I said, "Yeah, it should be good."

The ride back to my family's campsite was not totally awful; I didn't cry too much.

In later years, my dad said that he remembered that later that night I talked about the volleyball game in a strange, grandiose way. He said I was too stuck on how well I had played volleyball. That night, Saturday, I slept about five hours in our tent. I normally slept eight or nine. I was in a mixed mood. Part manic, part depressed.

Sunday, we got home from the mountains at about nine o'clock at night. I had to wake up Monday, June 27 at 5:00 a.m. to get to the airport by 6:00 a.m.

I had to unpack from camping and pack for Israel. I was hyper by that time. Two of my poker buddies, Jim Eckhart and Ed Lundblad, came over to say good-bye. I was so hyper and manic and busy trying to figure out what to pack that I didn't notice when they put a folding chair in my suitcase as a joke. I was that distracted. They were laughing, and so was I, because I was just a bit manic. I finally got packed and they left at about eleven thirty.

Still, I stayed up until about two in the morning to figure out some stuff I had to send in to UPS for school. I slept from 2:00 a.m. to 5:00 a.m. That lack of sleep would be a problem.

We got to the airport, and everyone who was going from the Seattle area was there. There were a bunch of us. We got on a plane for New York that was loaded with JTG members. My mood at that point was just a little bit hyperactive. It was a fun plane ride to LaGuardia Airport.

Orientation took place at a hotel. Brian Green, an acquaintance from Seattle, started hanging around with me. At some point Brian and I walked to a restaurant for dinner with a few girls from Seattle. Later, there was a big orientation meeting at a hotel, where they played "The Star-Spangled Banner." This got my attention because it reminded me of swim meets. The big point of the orientation meeting was that if you used drugs in Israel, you would be sent home. They spent about a half hour telling us this.

My mind was filled with distressing thoughts—part manic and part depressed.

Then there were religious services with just our group number six. There were about eight different groups of about sixty kids each. Brian wanted to skip services.

I said, "No, let's go to services."

He complained that I never wanted to do what he wanted to do. Anyhow, we went to services.

We took a bus to Kennedy Airport. There, I was in a much more jovial mood. Thinking funny, optimistic thoughts preoccupied me so badly that I needed Brian's help to figure out which counter to go to in order to pick out a seat on the plane. At one point, there was a JTG official who saw Brian and I eating non-kosher hot dogs while wearing JTG nametags. (They were non-kosher because they were pork.)

He said, "That's inconsistent."

I said to Brian, laughing, "Hey, we're inconsistent." I laughed some more, and so did Brian. We thought it was hilarious.

"We're inconsistent," we laughed. "We're inconsistent."

Later, I was nervous going through the security check of my luggage. I was fearful of going to a war zone. My suitcase was a mess because of the way I packed.

The security guard asked, "Is this the way you packed?"

I said, "Yes."

"Do you recognize anything that is not yours?"

I looked at a couple of shirts there and had to think a minute if they were mine. I had just bought them and didn't immediately remember that they were mine.

After a minute, I said, "No. It's all mine."

Being questioned made me nervous, but that particular nervousness went away when I got on the plane.

On the plane, I sat next to a window on my left and a girl and a guy to my right. I just sat in a smiling, near laughing stupor. I just sat there laughing and smiling almost the whole flight. Part of what I was thinking was that I could tell what people were thinking by the expression on their faces because I had so much practice with my mom. My mom could only shake her head "Yes" or "No," say "Dee" in sentences, and let us guess the expression on her face. I thought this face reading technique was a good way to pick up girls. I wasn't laughing out loud, just to myself. This was a symptom of mania. I thought I could read people's thoughts in great detail. It was a ten-hour flight non-stop from New York to Tel Aviv. The flight left about midnight the night of Monday the 27th, and got to Israel about 6:00 p.m. on Tuesday the 28th. You have to add eight hours for the time zone change. I, however, was so out of it, I thought it was Wednesday when we landed.

For a while on the plane, the flight attendants wanted us to keep the shades pulled down on our windows. This was to allow people to sleep. Being manic, I, of course, didn't sleep.

I said to the girl next to me, "They don't want us to see the fighter planes out there."

I was serious, and I'm sure she thought I was crazy, but she didn't say anything. We were still over the Atlantic, which shows I had no sense of time. Darren Gollub, our tour leader from Seattle, had told us that Israel-bound airliners are sometimes given fighter escorts. Of course, this is only over the Mediterranean and not the Atlantic. In my mind, I was imagining aerial combat, as I had seen in clips of Vietnam aerial combat: air-to-air missiles, aerial bombardment of ground targets, surface-to-air missiles, phantoms in formation, and so on. I really thought there might be some of this going on outside the window.

On the news about this time, there was a lot of talk about cults that used brainwashing to force people to join them. I had decided that Judaism was one big cult that was trying to keep me with them. I wasn't afraid of any coercion from JTG, but I thought they had played "The Star-Spangled Banner" at orientation deliberately to get my attention because they knew it would remind me of swim meets. I thought it was a psychological trick.

I knew Judaism was escapable, yet there seemed to be a conspiracy going on.

I tried to say "This is amazing," to Darren Gollub, a group leader from Seattle, who was leading another group in Israel. He was on the plane too, but later he told me I had mumbled, so he didn't understand me.

When the sun rose and we lifted the shades, we could see nothing but blue sky. That minimized my air battle fears at the time. I still looked for other planes, though.

We landed in Israel, and everybody cheered. Then as we were getting off the plane, I was feeling rather optimistic. I felt I could easily survive six weeks as a tourist. I said, "Well, it looks like we're in Israel, and it is Wednesday, and it is a nice day."

The two people near me said, "No, it's Tuesday. It's Tuesday."

I said, "No, no. It's Wednesday."

One of them said, "No, it's Tuesday. It's just ten hours plus eight for the time zone."

I said, "No, no. It's Wednesday."

They just gave me a funny look and gave up.

We were in the baggage claim area when one of our tour leaders asked if anyone had not turned over his passport and plane ticket to them for safekeeping. I hadn't, so I brought up my carry-on flight bag and started searching through it for my passport and ticket.

As I was searching my flight bag, a uniformed female security guard wearing a walkie-talkie came up and grabbed my ticket out of my hand and asked, "Are you going to Copenhagen?"

I said, "Huh?"

She said, "Are you going to Copenhagen?"

"What?"

"Are you going to Copenhagen?"

"What?"

"Are you going to Copenhagen?"

"Oh, uh, yeah, on the way back we stop in Copenhagen."

"Have a nice trip," she said as she handed my ticket back.

I freaked out. I knew that I had just matched the profile of a disturbed person in an Israeli airport. In Israeli airports, they are looking for terrorists. I knew that I was upset about a lot of things and that I didn't feel normal. Even though I may have had a smile on my face, I'm sure I looked hyper and nervous. Now I was worried about myself.

I found Debbie Frish (sister of my poker friend Dave Frish) who was in our group and said to her, "Don't play cards with me." She just looked surprised and said nothing.

I said again, "Don't play cards with me."

Debbie just looked surprised and annoyed and then said, "Okay, I won't play cards with you."

I said, "No, you see my mom can't talk, she had a stroke and it's buggin' the hell out of me. We can tell what she's thinking only by the expression on her face, so nobody can bluff me."

Debbie said something reassuring that helped for a minute. Somebody else put my suitcase on the bus, and we were off to Haifa.

When I got on the bus, Brian slid over to make room for me to sit down, so I felt obligated to sit with him. I told him that my mom not being able to talk to me was really bothering me.

Brian said, "You should talk to our tour leaders about this."

I said, "Yeah, maybe," but I didn't want to look for them just then.

"You feel guilty about this."

"No."

"You feel guilty about it, like maybe you caused it."

"No, I'm just pissed."

Brian said, "Yes, you feel guilty."

I said loudly, "Green, would you listen? I don't feel guilty about anything. The problem is, people think I'm a little different because I don't listen to what they say. Instead, I just watch the expression on their faces because that's all we can do with my mother. This is a cold, cruel world. You don't think death and war is real? You don't think F-4 Phantom fighter-bombers are real? It's not just on TV you know?"

Brian was speechless.

I went on and on like this all the way from Tel Aviv to Haifa during the hour drive. I was talking loud, switching from topic to topic and saying inappropriate things.

I remember the point at which we got to our base, a school in Haifa. We got off the bus. I was still carrying on in a loud, inappropriate manner.

Then I finally shut up and sat at a table so our tour leaders could talk to all of us. People were crying because they knew I was losing my mind. Poor Brian didn't deserve all the yelling. Our tour leaders had planned some orientation for that evening but decided "everyone" was under too much stress.

This was a manic outburst, about which nothing good can be said.

We went up to our bedrooms. There were seven beds in the room. Brian grabbed a bed right next to mine. One guy tried to say something calming, but I was resistant.

Finally, we turned off the lights, and I said, "Let's tell some dirty jokes." A couple guys actually did.

Fortunately, I really slept that night, about six hours. In the morning while lying in bed, I imagined myself a great philosopher commenting on everything from love to Middle East politics. When I got up, I thought it was Thursday morning. It was actually Wednesday.

In the morning, there were religious services. I got there late and had forgotten my talis (prayer shawl), kepah (prayer skullcap), and prayer book. I felt nervous and out of place.

Then a girl sitting behind me gave me her prayer book and said, "Here." She was trying to be friendly, and it worked for the rest of services. I felt calmer. However, after services, I was lost in space again.

I spent that entire day in a fog. I remember only a few things. In the morning, we went for a walk to a bank. Everyone was hesitant to go up to a teller, but I went right up to one. I actually made my traveler's check out for the 31st of June instead of the 29th, but it was okay. The teller just gave me a weird look. There is no such day as June 31st. I remember

I didn't eat anything at lunch. I just stared into space. I guess people thought I was stoned on drugs.

Evening came, and I thought two days had passed, so I thought it was Friday evening, the start of the Sabbath. It was actually Wednesday. I refused to go to dinner or get out my bus fare. (We were going to go somewhere after dinner.) I thought our tour leaders were playing a trick on us by telling everyone it was Wednesday when it was actually Friday. In JTG groups, you observed the Sabbath strictly. This meant you didn't ride on a bus on Sabbath, and you didn't spend money on Sabbath. Spending money is like doing business. If you obey all the strict rules of Sabbath, you are supposed to rest and not do anything resembling business. Business is work. I thought I was the only one who had caught on to our tour leaders trick of saying it was Wednesday when it was Friday evening, the start of the Sabbath. All the other guys went down to dinner. When I asked them not to go, they thought I was crazy.

Also, the tour leader, Sam, who heard me ask them not to go, got really mad.

He said, "Now I'm really getting pissed at you!"

I said, "It's Friday. It's the Sabbath."

He said, "No. It's Wednesday!"

Brian said, "It's Wednesday! What would your dad say?"

I said, "Forget that."

They went down to dinner.

Sam came up to my room a couple of times and asked me to come down to dinner. I found out later that he had concluded that I was on LSD, the hallucinogenic street drug. I refused to go down to dinner and told him I was looking through my luggage for my toothbrush.

Another tour leader, Ted, came up and into my room and said, "What kind of drugs are you on?"

I said, "I'm not on drugs."

He said, "Last night you were on some."

"Flying on that plane was a wild experience," I said, momentarily remembering that only one day had gone by.

"You're flying now"

"Yeah, right."

I had been fumbling with an injector razor, but I couldn't figure out how to inject the blade. I had never used that type before.

I said, "Would you do this for me?"

He put in the blade for me.

Then he asked, "What are you doing?"

"I'm looking for my toothbrush."

He went away for a while, and I went to the bathroom and shaved. Then Ted came back.

He said, "Why don't you come down and have dinner."

"I don't rush on the Sabbath."

"It's not the Sabbath. It's Wednesday the twenty-ninth."

He showed me his watch, and I looked at it, but I didn't know where to look to see the date. I thought he had set it back anyway as part of our tour leaders' game of seeing if anybody really knew what day it was.

Ted said, "What kind of drugs are you on?"

"None."

"C'mon, what kind of drugs are you on?"

Not to be argumentative, I jokingly said, "Let's see—cocaine."

Ted didn't take it as a joke, though. He believed me and said, "Did you read the rules?"

"Well, actually, I think I just signed them without reading them."

"Don't you think you should read before you sign?"

"Well, I know what the rules are. Why? Are you interviewing me?" I asked.

"Interviewing you for what?"

"For the job of JTG Israel Pilgrimage tour leader for next year," I said totally seriously. I thought they were interviewing me because I was the only one who had figured out their day-switching trick.

Then Ted went back downstairs.

I gave up on finding my toothbrush and finished getting dressed in clothes that were slightly nicer because I thought it was Sabbath. I went downstairs a few minutes later. Everyone else had already left for somewhere.

Then I saw Ted and caught him talking about me to a secretary who was down there. I heard Ted say, "And then he's got this razor thing that he doesn't know what to do with, and he thinks we're interviewing him."

Ted was laughing and thinking it was funny when I walked up and asked, "What are you doing?"

Ted looked flustered for a second and said, "Let me get you something to eat."

"I'm not hungry."

"C'mon, eat"

"No."

"C'mon, have some."

"Why?"

"We don't want you to skip meals."

"So?"

"C'mon," he said.

"Okay, fine," I said, disgusted.

He brought me a tray of food from the kitchen, and I started to eat. Then he asked me, "Is anything *bothering* you?"

I said, "Yes. *You're* bothering me."

"I'm your JTG group leader."

"You don't act like it," I said, as I started to eat.

"What do you mean?"

"You're not observing the Sabbath," I said, eating some more.

"It's Wednesday. What kind of drugs are you on?"

"I'm not on drugs."

"You said you were."

"I was just kidding," I said, taking some more food.

We talked a little more, and I finished eating. I started to walk out the door. Then Ted grabbed me suddenly by the arm to stop me from going. I broke away from his grip. I wondered why he was starting to get rough but waited for him anyway. He spoke to someone in the kitchen in Hebrew too fast for me to understand.

Then Ted started talking in Hebrew outside to a middle-aged man who, I theorized, was a member of a right-wing Israeli extremist organization. I thought they were planning to force me to join the extremist organization. I thought they wanted to brainwash me into helping them fight the Palestinians and other Arabs.

Ted and the middle-aged man quit talking and the man said to me, "I am your friend."

I punched him in the nose medium strength. I thought: *Get away from me, asshole. I'll decide who my friends are.*

Then I walked over to the open gate to the street and started to walk through it, but the security guard shut it. The guard said in an accented voice, "Too morrow, too morrow you will go out."

I made some half-hearted attempts to climb over the fence, but the guard pulled me down.

I thought this must be a concentration camp simulation exercise. Many Israelis were survivors of the Nazi Holocaust against the Jews, so I thought that now these racist Israelis were holding me prisoner as an initiation. I said to Ted, "This isn't funny. I want to go for a walk."

Ted said, "No." Then he started to talk to the middle-aged man and another man in Hebrew. I was thinking, *Here are some racist, right-wing extremist, militaristic, Jewish Israelis who think Jews are the master race, and they are going to try to force me to join them. They want to brainwash me into helping them kill Arabs. Being an Israeli is like being a Nazi. They are so racist. They think intermarriage is a crime.*

I thought about Melanie and Katie.

I was thinking, *If only the rest of the American kids would get back here and help me.*

Giving the Nazi salute, I yelled to the men there, "They were all saying Heil Hitler, Heil Hitler, but you knew they were full of shit! They were all saying Heil Hitler, Heil Hitler, but you knew the invasion was coming!" I went on like this for a while. The men stopped speaking in Hebrew and looked at me for a second. I stopped speaking, and then they started back up again in Hebrew. I couldn't understand Hebrew when spoken quickly.

I started up again, "They were all going Heil Hitler, Heil Hitler, but you knew they were wrong!" I went on like this for a while.

One man (there were now several men) said, "How can you say this about a man to whom I lost twelve cousins, three aunts, and a brother?"

I pointed to each of the men present and said, "Nazi, Nazi, Nazi, Nazi, Nazi, Nazi."

This prompted more talk in Hebrew, and then four of them grabbed me and tried to drag me inside. I struggled, but they managed to get me inside. I didn't punch any of them because there were too many of them. When I was inside, they said I should go up to my room, but I wouldn't go. I continued to call them Nazis. After a while, I was afraid they were going to beat me up because I called them Nazis. They wouldn't let me walk away. Four of them grabbed me and dragged me into a room. I would've killed them if I could have. None of the now ten men except Ted, who was in tears, were people I recognized. I thought I was being kidnapped.

As I was being dragged near the secretary, I said, "Call the police."

One of the men said, "Vee vill get you ze poleez."

In the room, there were ten men, so I was afraid to fight. I was horrified. I thought they were going to beat me up and torture me. It would be like being a prisoner of war, only nobody would know where I was. America did not know that Israel was capturing people like this. At least during the Vietnam War, we knew the names of most of the people who were captured, and we knew that they were somewhere in Vietnam. My captors made me sit in a chair. There were three of them standing really close to me and seven others in a small room. They were all looking at me and talking in angry, hurried tones to each other about me in Hebrew, which I did not understand. I was so scared that they did not even have to hold my arms when they gave me a shot of a drug, which I have since learned was the sedating, antipsychotic Thorazine. I thought the shot was to brainwash me into joining them in their fight against Palestinians and other Arabs.

I woke up in an ambulance, tied to a stretcher.

I said, "All I'm going to do is live. All I'm going to do is live." I meant that as long as they let me live, I would cooperate.

One of the men in the ambulance kept saying, "Nobody is trying to hurt you. Nobody is trying to hurt you."

I thought, *Yeah bullshit, then why are you kidnapping me? Where are the U.S. Marines when you need them? Will the United States go to war with Israel to save me? Israel could just report I died to cover up my capture.*

The ambulance stopped and they pulled me out on the stretcher. I looked over my shoulder and saw a sign that said *Rambam Hospital.* (The signs there are often in both Hebrew and English.) I thought, *What are they taking me to a hospital for?*

Then there were people surrounding me wearing white coats and speaking in Hebrew. I was too intimidated and drugged to say anything.

Next I was in an elevator, and then I saw a sign that said *Psychiatric Ward.*

I thought psychiatric wards were for murderers. Did I murder anybody? No! Then I thought, *Wait, the Soviet Union puts political prisoners in psychiatric wards. Israel must do so also. I'm a political prisoner!*

The next thing I knew I woke up from what seemed like a good sleep. My contact lenses had been in overnight, so my eyes felt thick and dry. I took my lenses out and tried to find something to put them in. An orderly took them, and I panicked. I was afraid he didn't know what they were. I was afraid they didn't have contact lenses in Israel. I was motioning to my eye and then this other guy with blonde hair said, "Hard or soft?"

I was so relieved. They knew what contacts were enough to say "Hard or soft." I also felt for a minute or so that JTG was taking good care of me because I hadn't been sleeping well.

When the guy with the blonde hair said, "Hard or soft?" though, I thought that meant he knew English very well, and I could talk to him like I would talk to an American. This was a mistake. A few minutes later he took me into a room to talk to me. He said with only a mild accent, "I am Dr. Ancell."

I said, "Hi."

He asked a lot of stuff, including, "Do you take pills? Are you on any medication?"

I said, "No."

"Your father was against this trip?"

"Well, uh, yeah."

I don't remember the whole conversation, but several times he said, "Talk slow, I don't understand when you speak so fast."

I thought he was trying to tell me to relax and not be nervous. I didn't understand that he meant he really had trouble understanding me. His English was not really very good. I knew he was a psychiatrist at this point, and I thought he just wanted me to relax.

He said, "Your mother is sick, and that bothers you?"

At first I thought he meant something else happened to her. I said, "Really, what happened?"

"She is crippled and can't speak."

I said, "Oh, yeah, that's right, she can't." It felt good to talk to a psychiatrist. I don't remember what all I said. I had heard of psychiatrists and counseling before, but I didn't really know anything about them.

Later he said, "We'll talk more later."

I remember saying I wanted to leave.

An orderly named Greg kept following me around as I looked for an exit, saying, "The doctor will decide when you can go."

I kept saying, "The doctor has decided." Thinking of myself as the doctor, as the captain of my own ship.

The next thing I remember, I was sitting on a table in a small room on a different ward. I was arguing with the people there and calling them Nazis. They took my blood pressure and then forcibly gave me an injection with the sedating, calming, antipsychotic Thorazine to put me to sleep.

There were usually about four people surrounding me when I was yelling, otherwise I might have started punching. I still felt I was a political prisoner. I thought I might be in this hospital for life. I thought that if I was not going to be in here for life, then maybe they wanted to make me stay in Israel for life. There is no way I wanted to stay in Israel for life.

One time when I was yelling, about eight male patients (it was an all-male ward) surrounded me and one said, "I'll kill you. I'll kill you."

Someone else said, "You must come with us."

They forced me over to my bed and started taking off my pants. I thought they were going to rape me. I yelled, "Greg!"

He told them to stop touching me, but then he gave me an injection of antipsychotic Thorazine in my butt. It put me to sleep.

About the only time manic depressives might get violent is when they are being forced into treatment. When you are manic, you feel fine and don't think there is anything wrong with you; therefore, you don't see any need for treatment.

On one of the first few days, Dr. Ancell showed me the showers. In Nazi Germany, poison gas showers were used to kill Jews. When Ancell showed me the showers, I thought that he was saying that the Israeli racist Jews could kill me, an American Jew, if they wanted to. I was in their control, and I had to do what they said. I knew it was a regular shower because I had already used it, but it still felt like a death threat.

After a few days, the antipsychotic Thorazine had made me sleep enough to be calm enough to cooperate with the staff. I started taking the drug in pill form when they told me to.

However, there was this huge muscular homosexual patient who kept harassing me. He kept wanting to borrow my shoes because they were Adidas. Adidas were imported to Israel, and so they were expensive. He also liked shaking my hand with a very strong grip, and once in a while he would make sexual suggestions.

I would say, "No, you do that with girls."

He then would smile and say, "Oh, yes."

There was one female aide I liked to talk to, but she didn't know much English. She would sometimes say, "I don't understand," but because she said it in English, I thought she knew English.

Eventually, after a few days, I started using the Hebrew I had learned at Mercer High.

One of the first things I remembered how to say was, "I don't know

Hebrew," in Hebrew. This would confuse the patients and the staff into thinking I knew Hebrew because I said it in Hebrew. Being in the hospital like this was an intensive crash course in Hebrew under duress. I had to remember all the Hebrew I had ever known, or life would be more difficult. Eventually I figured out there were two options: either I speak to them in Hebrew and they speak to me in English, or I speak to them in English slowly, using big pauses between each word, no big words, and no slang. They would usually respond in English. I didn't get this really mastered until about July 5.

A typical exchange went something like this:

I said very slowly, "When do we get our snack?"

"Ten o'clock," said an Israeli patient.

"Is it always bread and tea?"

"Yes."

At first, when I could have a conversation that successful, I was happy. That was progress over the first few days.

I still had some delusions. The staff played the radio for us sometimes. The radio played American rock and roll. There was Fleetwood Mac's "Don't Stop Thinking about Tomorrow," which I thought meant I could get out of the hospital tomorrow. This conflicted with "Hotel California" by the Eagles with the lines, "We are prisoners here of our own device," and "You can check out any time you like, but you can never leave." Early on, I thought the Haifa municipal radio station played these songs specifically for me, to give me a secret message. This is the first time I ever heard the song, "Hotel California."

The psychiatric ward was a strange place. One patient there went quickly through everyone's dresser drawers, ransacking them.

I said, "Hey, what are you doing?"

He said, "Shut up!" in a threatening tone, so I shut up.

Later, I figured he was having nicotine fits and was looking for cigarettes. Now, I think he was manic in addition to suffering from nicotine withdrawal. I've never seen such a nicotine fit.

Another guy was in for what I guess was extreme depression. He couldn't shave himself, so somebody was doing it for him.

Around July 2, a staff person said, "Your father is coming here."

I said, "Really? Wow."

A couple of days later, I realized by talking with the other patients that I would get out eventually, if I cooperated. I figured I had better cooperate or I could be given electroshock or a lobotomy like in the movie *One Flew Over the Cuckoo's Nest*. My dad came that day, and I pretended to be glad to see him, thinking that if we appeared to be getting along, I would get out sooner. I still had some fear of a conspiracy to hold me against my will indefinitely, so it was good that my dad wanted me out of there. We talked for about ten minutes.

I told my dad, "You are the father of the problem."

He said, "What?"

"You are the father of the problem."

"You're kidding me, Bill, aren't you?"

"Just forget it."

Another thing my dad said was, "Your doctor says you're doing better today."

This made me try to think of who my doctor was because at times the staff all blurred together. At times, all the patients and staff blurred together because they almost all had dark curly hair, dark complexions, spoke Hebrew, and smoked cigarettes. To this day, hot temperatures plus cigarette smoke reminds me of that hospital. My dad's comment about my doctor was helpful because it reminded me that Dr. Ancell was my doctor, and I started paying closer attention to him. I did get out of the Israeli hospital sooner because my dad was there. A funny thing is, I found out later that Dr. Ancell was from Mexico, so if I would've taken Spanish in high school, it could have been useful. His first language was Spanish. I had switched from Spanish to Hebrew in tenth grade, partly because I figured that as a Jew, I would have more use for Hebrew than Spanish. Little did I know.

Dr. Ancell and I needed to communicate better because for a long time he thought I was hearing voices, having auditory hallucinations.

He had asked me, "Are you hearing people speak to you?"

I said, "Yes, I'm hearing my friend say 'have a good time'—also my aunt, also Jim Eckhart saying 'Don't do anything I wouldn't do.'"

I just thought Ancell meant "hearing" in the sense meaning "remembering what people have said." It didn't occur to me that he was asking if I was having auditory hallucinations. However, from my response, he decided that I was having auditory hallucinations. I found this out much later.

I communicated well with one patient. He had lived in California for one summer, so he knew English well. He interpreted for me a few times when I was speaking to other patients or the staff.

While in the hospital, I longed for something familiar, even my calculus book. I felt this sure was a long way from Melanie Carson's arms. And it was no way to start out life as an adult and high school graduate.

On July 5, my dad said we might be leaving on July 7. That was hopeful. Most of my paranoid symptoms were gone by then. The antipsychotic Thorazine they had given me, at first in shots and then in pills, had worked. And my delusions about reading the expressions on people's faces were gone also.

On July 7, we left early in the morning. Fortunately, my dad was good at trying to get me the best medical care available when I was acutely sick. It was a good thing that he had enough money to pay Dr. Ancell to fly all the way back to Seattle with us. That way Ancell would be sure I was okay on the plane on the way back, and he could talk to the doctor I would start to see in Seattle.

It was a long flight, but it was sure good to be back in America. It was good to hear people speaking English and to see a variety of hair colors and encounter some people who weren't smoking. I would have preferred to rejoin my tour group, but they wouldn't take me back. We switched planes in New York and flew to Seattle from there. I was glad to be on a plane loaded with Americans. I was very glad to be back in America, even if it meant being in a psychiatric ward.

We went home to my house after we got to Seattle. My brothers and my mom were very relieved to see that I was okay.

I said, "Ahnee low meshugana, ahnee American." That's Hebrew for, "I'm not crazy. I'm American."

My brothers were relieved that I was making sense.

Then we went to Helgerson Hospital in downtown Seattle. I was put in the psychiatric ward and met Dr. Ronald Kelly. I begged him to let me show him that I could fall asleep without drugs, but he insisted on giving me some antipsychotic Thorazine. As it turns out, I did need the Thorazine or an antipsychotic of some kind. It was what Dr. Ancell had been giving me in Israel, and for the short-term it was good medical practice. I was on Thorazine for three months.

Dr. Kelly and Dr. Ancell then had plenty of time to talk to each other. Ancell had flown all the way back to Seattle with us from Israel, at my dad's request and expense.

I slept that night, and I woke up in the morning. The hospital in America was much nicer than in Israel. I had my own room rather than having to share it with five other guys. Also, the food was better, with familiar brands of familiar foods in familiar wrappers, written in English. Not so much yogurt, eggs, and greens. More meat and potatoes. Land o' Lakes butter and milk. Wheaties. Corn Flakes. Cheerios.

I participated in occupational therapy, better described as arts and crafts. It was led by nice American women who all obviously thought I was sicker than I was. They talked baby talk to me until I talked to them for a while. I found out later that they had been told that I was hallucinating regularly. When I read my chart years later, I saw they wrote that they observed me having some hallucinations. They were mistaken. The way I moved my eyes or something made them think I was seeing things. Some manics hallucinate; others don't. I'm one who doesn't.

Earlier I had been asked, "Are your poker friends with you in the hospital?"

I said, "Yes," but I meant they were with me in spirit and that they wanted me to get better. It hadn't occurred to me that they were asking if I was having visual hallucinations.

Their idea that I was having hallucinations was a mistake. It is a serious symptom that I didn't have, and I don't want to be thought of as having had them. It does not necessarily change the diagnosis, because some manics do hallucinate. However, the doctors need to know if you are hallucinating because if you are, you are more likely to be diagnosed schizophrenic. Manic depression and schizophrenia are different from each other, and the treatments are different, so health care professionals need to get the story straight. Sometimes manic people know what they are seeing is not real, and sometimes they do not know. However, they could have told me to point to where my poker friends were sitting right then, name them, say who was dealing, say what game they were dealing, and tell what I had just bet.

I would have said, "Are you guys crazy? Why are you asking me all these bizarre questions?"

When thinking back to that time, I didn't see or hear anything out of place. I could have only hallucinated some very ordinary pieces of furniture in very ordinary places.

Of course, I had plenty of delusions. Delusions are ridiculous conclusions drawn from normal sights and sounds. The flight attendant wanted the shade down, so I thought she was hiding fighter planes. Some men thought I was acting strangely as a tourist in Israel, so I thought they wanted to kidnap me and brainwash me. The Haifa municipal radio station played "Hotel California," and I thought they were sending me a personally harassing secret message like, "Our minds are definitely twisted," from the words of the song.

For a while, I kept up the mistaken attitude that although I had been confused, most of the problem I had in Israel resulted from a misunderstanding due to the language barrier. I didn't know I had a definable illness. I just thought I had been under too much stress and had not gotten enough sleep.

On July 15, 1977, I was discharged from the hospital with no current delusions, but I didn't know that I had been out of touch with reality. I knew I had been confused about which day it was, but I thought the whole thing had largely been a misunderstanding because the group leaders had wrongfully accused me of being on street drugs, and because I didn't know Hebrew.

Dr. Kelly had, up to this point, failed to tell me my diagnosis. I had asked, "What's wrong with me?"

He had said, "Oh don't worry, we'll have you out of here soon." He wouldn't answer the question.

Many years later, in 1989, I requested a copy of my medical records, and I saw that he had written in 1977 that I was schizophrenic. He failed to tell me that, even though I had asked him directly. I consider that awful, even if it was a bad guess at diagnosis. The patients' bill of rights in effect in most states requires that a patient know his or her diagnosis. He also got the diagnosis wrong to begin with. I consider that bad medical practice.

Dr. Kelly's failure to diagnose correctly—and his failure to discuss the diagnosis with me—delayed the beginning of my recovery from 1977 to 1982. I was properly diagnosed and started getting better care in 1982. I started cheering up then.

Years of manic depressive misery could have been minimized if Dr. Kelly had recognized that I was manic depressive and had told me that I was manic depressive. Also, I would need antidepressants in just a few months, but Dr. Kelly never prescribed them or told me that they existed. I had never heard of antidepressants. I experienced a lot of depression and mania during future years that could have been avoided with antidepressants and antipsychotics. Dr. Kelly could have told me how to recognize mania in myself, and it would have prevented a lot of problems, including two hospitalizations. If he had told me about antidepressants, I likely would have graduated from college in four years instead of six, and I likely would've had a better social life. He never talked to me about my symptoms.

I didn't hear about antidepressants and didn't realize that they would help me until February 1982. When I realized how much they helped and that Dr. Kelly had failed to mention them, I wanted to sue him for medical malpractice. However, the doctor I had then was unwilling to testify against Dr. Kelly, so I was unable to sue. I now have the medical records from this 1977 episode. In the records, Dr. Kelly also complains that I hadn't admitted that I was mentally ill. That was not true.

I had asked him, "What is wrong with me?" I had also asked, "What is my diagnosis?"

He never answered.

Dr. Kelly never discussed my symptoms with me. He never named any mental illness that I was supposed to think I had. He never named any illness I was supposed to admit I had. As a result of his lack of information, I thought I was just confused from not sleeping enough.

He never even said the words "mentally ill" to me. Another problem is that he would often, in the hospital, treat me like a baby.

For example, when I was feeling better, I would ask, "Tell me why I can't get out today. How long will I be here?"

He would say, "There, there, now, everything will be okay." He wouldn't answer the question. This clearly indicated his intent of never carrying on a rational conversation with me. My barber and my dentist talk to me more than my psychiatrist, Dr. Kelly, ever did.

This was his chance to start a rational, intelligent discussion with me about what had gone on. Instead, he never discussed the incidents in Israel when something went drastically wrong with me. Discussing these incidents and the months before was essential for making a proper diagnosis. He never did. It doesn't take a legal or medical genius to know that it was Dr. Kelly's duty to ask me what I was thinking and why I was doing what I was doing in Israel and the months before. He also never asked if I had any family members with mental illness. Asking that would have also helped. He should have asked my dad that, and my dad would have told Dr. Kelly that my mom had manic depression. Manic depression has a strong genetic component.

He never asked these questions.

Dr. Kelly did continue the antipsychotic Thorazine, which for the short-term was decent medicine.

Throughout this book, medications will always be preceded by adjectives like "antipsychotic" or "antidepressant." I want the types of medications I discuss to be crystal clear. At times, they will not be living up to their descriptions. Often they will fail because the doctor made errors in the prescribing strategy. At other times, they will fail because they are far from perfect under the best of circumstances. By the end of the book, the drugs are successful. Medication becomes the hero of this book.

CHAPTER 8

DR. KELLY PRETENDS TO PRACTICE OUTPATIENT PSYCHIATRY

I went to a poker game with my usual friends and said something like, "I'd like to tell you guys what happened, but I'm not really sure."

I left the card game relatively early to make sure I got enough sleep. I wondered what my friends had been told about me, but I didn't have the assertiveness to ask. I was afraid that they had heard only an official fifth-hand rumor, and I didn't know what the rumor was.

I was on a lot of antipsychotic Thorazine, so it was hard to talk, and I still had heard nothing about my diagnosis. I hadn't figured out what had gone wrong the night they put me in the hospital.

I told some people that the explanation for the events in Israel was that I was confused. I said mostly it was a misunderstanding from the language barrier and from the Israelis thinking that I was on drugs. I said I was also confused because I hadn't slept much in five days. It's true I hadn't slept much in the five days prior to being put in the hospital, but that was as much a symptom as a cause. I figured it was nervous exhaustion or stress.

I saw Dr. Kelly three times as an outpatient that summer. His treatment did not help me at all. I sat in a chair and talked, facing him. He just wrote down what I said. I saw him for a half an hour. Here is what a typical session with him was like.

At the beginning of the half hour he asked, "How are you?"

I then talked for five minutes. I told him about myself, Dad, Mom, my brothers, Melanie, school, Israel, swimming, or my friends. He wrote down what I said. He didn't say a word. He did not give me any information.

Then he asked, "How's your family?" Again, I spoke for about five minutes. I told him about myself, Dad, Mom, my brothers, Melanie, school, Israel, swimming, or my friends. He wrote down what I said. He didn't say a word. He did not give me any information.

Then he asked, "What have you been doing?"

I spoke for about five minutes. I told him I had been running, playing tennis, and playing poker. He wrote down what I said. He didn't say a word. He did not give me any information. After a few more general questions like this, the half-hour session was over.

He said, "Okay, time's up. Bye." At the time, I thought that was standard practice. I didn't know any better.

During my five-minute answers to his general questions, I displayed symptoms of depression from being dragged down by antipsychotic Thorazine. I also described symptoms of mania and depression from the recent past while answering his questions. However, Dr. Kelly apparently missed the significance of the symptoms I was describing. At that time, I didn't know they were symptoms of a specific disease. I hadn't heard of manic depression before, so I didn't know what it was. I know now.

Occasionally, with great effort, I could get Dr. Kelly to answer a question. I asked, "Why did they put me in the hospital the way they did? Couldn't they just have let me catch up on sleep? Couldn't they have told me that they wanted to take me to a hospital?"

After I asked him three times, he said, as if he was quite annoyed at the question, "You took a swing at the tour director."

When he said that, and after I had talked to many people other than Dr. Kelly, I became more sure that the people who dragged me into the room were not right-wing Israeli extremists trying to brainwash me into killing Arabs just because I was Jewish like them. Eventually, I figured out they must have been the cooks and janitors who worked at the school we were staying at, and one of them was the tour supervisor.

Eventually, by gathering information from people other than Dr. Kelly, and by thinking about it enough, I figured out what had happened. I did this by talking to a lot of people who had been on the trip, including Brian Green, when they got home. I realized that there was something seriously wrong with me. Also, I remembered the stress I was feeling from my home situation, and I figured that that was a major cause of the problem. So, I wanted a word for what happened, and all my dad would say was that I was "sick." He acted like it was outlandish for me to want another word that was more specific. I wondered if *nervous breakdown* was the word and asked some people what word they had heard, but nobody knew a specific word.

I asked Dr. Kelly, "What is the word for the problem I had in Israel?"

I paused, and Dr. Kelly remained expressionless in his chair. He kept writing.

I asked Dr. Kelly again, "What is the *word* for it?"

I paused. Dr. Kelly kept writing. He kept looking down at his yellow legal pad. He was ignoring me.

"Dr. Kelly, is there a *word* for it? Is there a *name* for the problem I had there? Dr. Kelly, is there a word for it? Is 'nervous breakdown' the word? *What's my diagnosis?*"

He finally acted startled, quit writing, sat up in his chair, adjusted his hearing aid, and said, "'Nervous breakdown' is not the word." He went on to say, "What happened to you has no known explanation, and it is very rare. All it can be called is a severe thinking disturbance." His tone was that of a spectator rather than a concerned caregiver. His tone seemed to be asking: What are you asking me for? He lied when he said that there was no word for it, after he had already written down a diagnosis. He had written that I was schizophrenic and that I would need medication for an indefinite period. I know that he wrote that because—as I've mentioned—in 1989 when I started to write this book I requested a copy of my medical records from 1977.

Schizophrenia was the wrong diagnosis, but he could have at least said, "Well, it is either schizophrenia or manic depression. I'm not sure." Actually, he could not honestly be sure of anything, because he never asked me what my symptoms were. There is a list of symptoms for both diseases, and a decent psychiatrist can judge if you have or had those symptoms and to what degree. He never showed me the symptom lists. He gave me medication for only three months instead of an indefinite period. I needed to know my diagnosis. There is literature to read about schizophrenia that can help a patient. However, you will never find this literature if your doctor has not said the word "schizophrenia" to you. You won't know what to look under at the library.

At the library, I could have learned that schizophrenics usually hallucinate, don't have trouble sleeping, have their delusions and hallucinations in the presence of a normal mood, may have no emotional fluctuations at all, think that outside forces are controlling their mind (not just giving messages), or think that they can broadcast their thoughts. All of these symptoms would have helped rule out schizophrenia in my case. Maybe I would have read about manic depression in the same section of a book. Instead, Dr. Kelly lied by saying that he couldn't imagine a diagnosis.

Maybe he thought hearing the word "schizophrenia" would hurt my feelings. That would be redundant. My feelings could not have been hurt more than they already had been. I was already "a person who has been in a psychiatric ward." One more word would not hurt me. Sticks and stones may break my bones, but a diagnosis will never hurt me. It was very aggravating to hear basically, "There's no word for it."

If Dr. Kelly had been a good doctor, he would have questioned me closely about my episode and the months leading up to it. He would have discovered that I was manic depressive. Then he would have told me my diagnosis and tried putting me on mood-leveling lithium. Lithium is a treatment for manic depression. It is not a treatment for schizophrenia. He never prescribed this drug for me. He also should have told me about antidepressants. I would need antidepressants in a few months but didn't get them for four-and-a-half years, because Dr. Kelly failed to tell me about them. I didn't hear about them for four-and-a-half years. I suffered greatly because of his laziness.

As I said earlier, my barber and my dentist talk to me more than Dr. Kelly ever did.

At the back of this book is a list of symptoms of mania and depression that psychiatrists, psychologists, general physicians, social workers, and other people can use as a guide to recognize manic depression. People with the disease should seek treatment from a competent psychiatrist.

To qualify as manic or depressed, you usually need just four of these symptoms at the same time. To experience depression after a serious loss or other tragedy is normal, but the depression should last only two weeks or so. If it lasts longer, treatment is recommended.

Just for reference, a good doctor would have also talked to a few of my friends to find out my medical and psychological history. Dr. Kelly just talked to my dad. A doctor can't get an accurate psychological history of an eighteen-year-old by talking only to one parent. The doctor needs to talk to the patient's friends, with the permission of the patient, of course.

During that August of 1977, I needed something to do. It was summer. Classes at the University of Puget Sound didn't start until a few days after Labor Day. We were due for orientation a few days before Labor Day. In the meantime in August, I did some lawn work at home, hung out with my friends, and took a speed-reading course. The speed-reading course didn't work.

That summer, my friends stuck by me. I told them there had been something seriously wrong, but there was no explanation for it other than the stress from my family situation. I didn't know about the genetic aspects of it; I thought it was environmental.

Throughout the summer, I still thought of Melanie Carson and looked forward to being in the same city as her, Tacoma. In the same pattern as before my trip to Israel, I was hanging around, while being totally preoccupied with Melanie. I was now in the sort of depressive zone that the antipsychotic Thorazine drags you down into when it is trying to pull you down from mania. Mania is like being way too far up. Depressed is way too far down. Thorazine calms you down enough from mania to sleep at night, but it drags you down a bit during the day. It's sort of like depression. I was preoccupied with "I am a loser" thoughts.

The day before I left for college, Phil Holland and Jim Eckhart, two high school poker buddies, came over to say good-bye. We had been friends since we were little kids. I told my friends that I would visit and write. I felt like crying as they left my house. I had said good-bye to my other friends earlier. Some were going away, but many were living at home and going to UW.

CHAPTER 9

COLLEGE FRESHMAN
HALF THERE

During the ride down to the University of Puget Sound, I was alone in the car with my dad. I was sitting there not saying anything, and he was driving. He asked, "What are you thinking about?"

I said, "Nothing."

He put his foot on the brake and asked angrily, "Are you mad at me about something?"

Terrified at his threat of turning the car around, I said, "No, no," and I slid as far to the right in the passenger seat as I could.

"What are you thinking about then?" he asked, speeding up.

I said, "I'm thinking about what happened in Israel."

"What are you thinking about that for?" he asked angrily. "Are you afraid it's going to happen *again?*"

"No. I'm planning how to tell my roommates about it."

"You don't have to tell anybody about this."

"But I want to tell my roommates."

"What do you want to tell *them* for?"

"I'm planning on being *friends* with them."

He said angrily and loudly, "You don't need any friends! *I* never had any friends when *I* was in college!"

I said, "I want to have friends."

Taking his foot off the accelerator and slowing down, he said, "Maybe you're not *ready* to go to college yet. Maybe you should stay home."

I was shocked and horrified. I knew he was jealous of my potential relationship with my roommates. I said, "Okay Dad, fine. I won't tell them."

My dad then sped up a bit. Then there was a moment of silence, but he wouldn't leave me alone.

He asked, "What are you thinking about now? Are you still thinking about the *same thing?*"

"Yeah. Why?"

"Oh I'm taking you home!" he said angrily, taking his foot off the accelerator.

"I won't tell anyone."

"Okay, don't tell anyone," he said speeding up again.

"You don't need any friends other than me."

"Right, Dad, but I think I should be friends with my roommates."

"Oh, I'm taking you home!" he said angrily as he took his foot off the accelerator. He started looking for a place to turn the car around.

I said, "Okay, okay, Dad. I won't say a thing to them."

He sped up again.

He asked, "What did you want to tell *them* for?"

"They'll ask what I did this summer."

"Tell them to mind their own *business!*"

I said, "That wouldn't be very friendly. I want to be friends with them."

He said loudly and angrily, "What do you need friends for? I never had any friends when I was in college!"

This went on for a while, so to get him to keep driving, I told him I would not make any friends.

His yelling bothered me so much that I told my roommates, Wayne and Al, very little about my "severe thinking disturbance," as Dr. Kelly had called my manic episode. This violated the rule that says you tell your roommates about everything significant, whether it be good or bad, if you expect to be friends with them. One of my roommates from then, Wayne, is now a psychiatrist and was interested in psychology then. He could have suggested counseling then, and I might have gotten diagnosed earlier. I didn't take the initiative to go to counseling, because I felt I would've had to keep secret the fact that I was going and the reason I was going. At first I told my roommates that my medicine was for hay fever.

After a week or so, I told them, "Actually these pills aren't for hay fever. They're actually because when I was in Israel this summer, I hadn't been sleeping, so I kinda flipped out, so I have to take this medicine for a couple months, so I can sleep."

They said, "Oh, ok."

I tried to be as friendly to my roommates as possible. I told them the other things I did in the summer. We talked a lot about other stuff.

"What are you going to major in?" I asked.

"Maybe biology," said Wayne.

"Maybe physics," said Al.

"For me," I said, "Maybe physics or chemistry."

We kept talking about potential classes, what we had done in high school, where else we applied to college, our SAT scores, and lots of other stuff.

My roommates, Wayne and Al, were a little too polite and never pressed me for details of what had happened in Israel.

Wayne was from Olympia, and Al was from San Francisco. Wayne was interested in biology and psychology. In high school, Wayne had been on the debate team and had been a good student. Al was interested in computers and spent a long time in the computer center each day.

I soon returned to the depressed phase of manic depression. I was very unhappy. I tried to be as sociable as possible in an effort to cheer myself up. I was still depressed about my swimming performance in twelfth grade. Also, I was still depressed about not being the boyfriend of Melanie Carson.

I thought one day I would get my act together and I'd be able to call her at Pacific Lutheran University across town and say the right thing. However, she had said no to going to prom with me. I had asked her out again after prom in early June and she had said no to that also. By that time, she had probably heard that I had suffered a nervous breakdown. She would just say no again if I asked her out again. There was no point in calling her. I had bugged her too much as it was.

Few of the women at Puget Sound looked as good as I remembered her to be.

Thinking things would straighten out in my life, not knowing that I had a chronic illness, I decided to take pre-med classes. Many people at Puget Sound were pre-med, as were several of my poker buddies at home. I decided it was fashionable to be pre-med, so I'd be one too.

My concentration was poor. When I was alone and tried to study, I really had problems getting any schoolwork done. I would worry about swimming, about Melanie, about my "severe thinking disturbance" in Israel, and other things. It would take me three hours to do a one-hour assignment. The thoughts dominating my head went something like this:

Here I am stuck at this crummy place. These women are ugly. They average about a three on a ten-point scale. None compare to Melanie Carson. This is a crummy place. I'm a loser. What am I going to do? This is a crummy place.

I had a string of thoughts like this between maybe every paragraph of reading homework. I really thought a romance was the only way to cheer up.

There is a phenomenon that occurs with depression. You don't smile. This makes you ugly. This makes other people not smile at you. That makes them ugly. The problem compounds itself. Things get worse. It is a vicious circle.

I was friends with my roommates and the people on my floor, but because I was depressed, nobody seemed as fun as people seemed when I was well. I ate meals with them, and we would try to make each other laugh, but I had a pretty low percentage of successful jokes. We went to movies together, partied together, and hung out in our dorm rooms and talked. There were a lot of interesting people on my floor. It was fun getting to know people from all over the region.

I got some okay grades because I took easy classes. Fall quarter ended a couple days before Thanksgiving. I went home. We had Thanksgiving with my aunt, uncle, and cousins, the Felbers.

I saw Dr. Kelly again. I asked him again what the cause of my problem in Israel was, and he basically shrugged his shoulders again. I accepted that as good medical practice at the time! As a result of what he said, I believed I had nothing definably wrong with me.

In the winter, I was on the swim team. I lettered for swimming the 1000-yard freestyle in meets. I had switched to freestyle because I was upset with how poorly I had done the year before in breaststroke in high school. Lettering did not boost my pride though. I latched onto the negative thought that the UPS team was very minor league. My high school's records were faster than the UPS school records.

In the spring, I felt that I should possibly tell my roommates and floor mates some of the details of my "severe thinking disturbance." I felt they would know me and understand me better if they knew. Yet it seemed stupid and negative to tell.

At the beginning of the school year, I had told my resident advisor, "I am on medication for a severe thinking disturbance. Without it, I kind of flip out. I'll be on it until the prescription runs out, and then I won't be on it anymore."

She said, "Okay," and she didn't question me further.

This was because as our resident advisor, she had asked us to tell her of any medication. Nobody else had heard me tell her. Now, I decided I needed help in deciding whether or not to tell any gory details to my friends. I decided to talk to her about it. I tried knocking on her door, but she was never home. I sent her a note through campus mail, saying I wanted to talk to her. I didn't say what about. I wanted to be sure to talk to her, but keep it confidential, not make it sound like an emergency, and not make it look like she necessarily would be able to convince me of what to do without really listening. All these requirements seemed huge at the time because I was severely depressed. I was not assertive enough to make this easier. I knew that the difference between telling and not telling could be a big deal. Maybe they could give me moral support, but maybe they would think less of me.

My resident advisor stuck her head in my dorm room when there were about three people standing there, and she said, "Bill, did you want to talk to me?"

I said, "Oh, uh, I don't need to talk to you anymore." This was not true, but I had to say that because then everyone would want to know what we talked about.

She said, "Okay." Then she left.

Predictably, Wayne then said, "What did you want to talk to her about?"

I said, "Oh, nothing."

After that, I was too unassertive to ask her to talk to me again. I figured I already had bugged her too much, even though I hadn't bugged her. I knew that the happy me of old—who should be the present happy me—would have handled the situation tactfully, efficiently, and gracefully. I knew the "severe thinking disturbance," and the present unhappiness making it difficult to talk about, were related, but I did not know how. I could not imitate the happy me. I didn't know that my unhappiness was due to a definable disease. I thought it was due to my environment. I thought my crummy home environment was bugging me long distance, and I thought my lack of a girlfriend at college was a natural justifiable reason for feeling down.

Wondering what the happy me would be doing was a legitimate medical question, but it was also a symptom. All day I hesitated to move because I wondered what the happy me would be having for lunch, what the happy me would be saying right now, what the happy me would be studying right now, and what the healthy me would have been studying five minutes before. This could ruin a whole day and was a symptom.

That year I got a B average by taking several courses that I almost could have tested out of because I had learned the material in high school when I was well. I learned just a little bit in college. I couldn't concentrate; my mind was too filled with depressive, obsessive, negative, pessimistic thoughts.

It was a very sad and boring time.

CHAPTER 10

SUMMERTIME AND I CAN'T CHEER UP

The summer of 1978, I got a job as a lifeguard and swim instructor at the Mercer Island Jewish Community Center. It was an okay job, but my attention was not always what it should have been because I was depressed. When life guarding, I made a point of keeping my eye on the pool at all times like I was supposed to, but my mind was often elsewhere. I'm lucky nobody drowned.

I only worked about twenty hours a week because when I tried to work more I felt "stressed out" as I called it.

Feeling crummy at work and elsewhere, I felt I had to do something to make myself feel better. In my free time, I read self-help books. I read *How to Be Your Own Best Friend*, *Looking Out for #1*, *Your Erroneous Zones*, *Grief*, and *How to Take Charge of Your Life*. I liked reading these books. They seemed to be on my side in my conflict with my dad. However, my mood remained depressed after I read them. In other words, these books didn't help. They may help some people, but they didn't help me. They didn't help me regain the smoothness, happiness, or confidence I once had.

I did read one book that would eventually prove useful. It was *The*

Hite Report of Female Sexuality. It gave lots of good information about lovemaking. I also read *Cosmopolitan* magazine, to help me figure out women.

I didn't consider seeing a psychiatrist, because I had concluded psychiatrists couldn't really do anything. This conclusion was based on my experience with Dr. Kelly. I figured I was sleeping fine, so I didn't need the antipsychotic Thorazine—so I didn't need Dr. Kelly.

I went out with a few women that summer. Going on dates cheered me up for a couple of days at a time, but they didn't feel as delightful as I felt they should have.

CHAPTER 11

SOPHOMORE SPACE CADET

I spent most of the school year of 1978–1979 in my dorm room preoccupied with inappropriately negative, inappropriately pessimistic, depressive thoughts. I listened to lots of music in an effort to cheer myself up. The music helped only a bit.

In my classes that year, I got two Fs, one B, and the rest Cs. My grade average was below C level. I declared economics as a major because it was something I could use without graduate school. I didn't do much dating, because I was not well-liked. I didn't smile, and I was embarrassed about my grades.

I felt that I was such a loser that if a girl liked me, that would just prove she was stupid. With a stupid girlfriend, I would be miserable. If we broke up, I would be even more depressed. Breaking up is hard to do.

CHAPTER 12

INTRODUCTION TO GETTING FIRED

Summer came and I went back home. My dad got me a high-paying construction labor job. He was the friend of an executive in the construction company.

I worked as a construction laborer at a new maximum-security prison they were building. I tore apart wooden forms for concrete after the concrete was dry. Sometimes the forms were partly buried from rain, so we would have to dig to get them out. Other times the job involved carrying big girders from one place to another. Early on, my foreman got the idea that I didn't like him. I guess it was because I didn't smile at him or talk to him much. He transferred me to the supervision of another foreman. I had no idea why I was transferred. I thought the other foreman just needed the help. Then, the other foreman didn't like my attitude or productivity level, either. I found that out later. These were more symptoms of my depression. My work and the people I knew and worked with didn't seem fun. This was the "nothing is fun" phenomenon of depression.

A coworker of mine named Ron once asked me, "Do the students at the University of Puget Sound all have high intelligency?"

I said, "Intelligency is not a word."

I was such a jerk.

Another example of my bad mood occurred when Ron and I were shoveling off a foundation that had gotten covered with mud. At that time, a guy who I now suspect was spying on me for management, came and watched. A few minutes later, I slipped in the mud and fell on my back.

Then George, the guy who I thought came to spy, said in a friendly tone, "You aren't going to get a lot done lying on your back."

Ron said, "Yeah, that's what I keep telling him."

I got up, and George said, in a friendly tone, "Your mother is going to have more laundry to do now that you fell."

I turned away and said nothing. I'm sure now that he thought I was being rude, when he was just joking around. I turned and thought that he was ridiculously silly for being so jovial and thinking everyone has a normal mother who does laundry. It would be so nice if I had a normal family again, but I thought George was way out of line. I didn't get how everyone could be so happy all the time. George must have felt slighted when I said nothing, and that, in retrospect, probably contributed to my getting fired for having a bad attitude.

The foreman told the supervisor, who told someone else, who told someone else, who told my father's friend, who told my father: "Bill has the worst work attitude I have ever seen." My father came home from work and told me this. It was the first time I had heard about them being unhappy with my work. I was so grumpy and unapproachable that they didn't even want to approach me to say that I was grumpy and unapproachable.

The next day I told my original foreman that if he didn't like how I was doing, he should tell me—yell at me even. I told him not to tell my father. I ended up working there for another couple of weeks before I got "laid off."

The foreman said, "We don't know if you or the dirt will go flying when you shovel."

CHAPTER 13

SATISFACTORY PROGRESS
TOWARD FLUNKING OUT

In the fall of 1979, I started my junior year at the University of Puget Sound. Once that quarter, I went to see one of the psychologists at school. My dad had wanted us all to get counseling to talk about my mother's stroke. I went once and talked about her stroke and how it affected my dad.

The psychologist asked if I had ever been to counseling before.

I said, "Yes."

I told her about the events leading up to my experience (manic episode) in Israel, the incident in Israel itself, and the aftermath. She asked how depressed I was then, and I said that I was not depressed. That's how little insight into my own condition I had.

Talking with the psychologist made me think about Melanie Carson, so I wrote to her at Pacific Lutheran University across town. I told her how mad my dad had gotten before our date in spring of 1977, and I told her how much I liked her. I wrote that I was quitting school and would never live with my dad again.

Melanie wrote back promptly and said she had heard about my mom's stroke in high school and that it must be hard to accept. Melanie also said that she had recently been diagnosed with a potentially crippling disease, but she had recovered from her first attack 99 percent and was able to do everything she had been able to do in the past. Melanie also said that she did not want to go out with me that but it was nothing personal and not my religion either. I was glad she wrote back, and I saved that letter for a number of years.

Getting back to my conversation with the psychologist, I thought that depression was something you had immediately following a seriously bad event. You felt like crying all day, and then you gradually cheered up. There was no recent seriously bad event. I didn't feel like crying all day, and I was not gradually cheering up. What I had was not going away, so I thought it couldn't be depression! I thought that my poor concentration was due to having no steady girlfriend. I was used to my unhappiness and thought it was normal for my particular life. I had a few good dates with a woman who lived on my floor, but it didn't cheer me up enough. The information from *The Hite Report* proved useful, but we did not develop a committed relationship.

I had a habit of going to the library to study, but being unable to concentrate on homework, I went over to the newspaper section of the library and read the newspapers from various cities. In the newspapers, there were crime stories. I think these crime stories fit in with my depressive view of the world as a crummy place.

That quarter I dropped the class *Introduction to Drama*, so *Market Structure and Pricing Policy* and *Intro to Film Arts* were my remaining classes. I got Ds on the mid-quarter tests in both. I was unable to concentrate or feel motivated. My mind was filled with too many depressive, obsessive worries. I decided, when I got those results back, to quit school, or at least take a year leave of absence. I told the school administration that I wanted to take a leave.

When I told the Assistant Dean of Students that I was flunking out due to poor concentration, she looked at my high school grades and my SAT scores and said, "There is no problem here."

Ideally, a more informed dean would have looked at my awful college grades and insisted that I have a couple meetings with a psychologist before I quit. The purpose of this would have been to check for clinical depression. Clinical depression is not that rare. There was a problem. I was flunking out because I couldn't concentrate. I was clinically depressed, and I didn't even know it. I thought my mental situation was "normal" for what I just thought happened to be my particular situation. The psychologist I had seen earlier that quarter may have been able to diagnose me. I, an uninformed twenty-year-old, didn't know that mental health professionals were of any value. I thought "depression" was not the word for my situation.

I decided not to tell anyone that I was quitting. I had some friends who would've tried to talk me out of it. Some might have even suggested counseling. I didn't think counseling would help. I didn't want anyone to try to talk me out of it, so that's why I didn't tell anyone until there were just a couple weeks of school left.

I had read so much about crime in the newspapers, and I had heard about enough criminal incidents on campus that I decided I wanted to be a cop. Four years of college were not necessary to become a cop. As a cop, I could do some good in the fight against crime. I could help put criminals in jail. The idea itself was not crazy, but I eventually became crazy and kept the idea. I felt I was having academic problems because school was boring, and I needed something exciting.

About this time, I started telling my friends that I would be quitting school and going to work somewhere. They seemed disappointed but didn't really try to talk me out of it. I think Wayne, my roommate during freshman and sophomore year, suggested counseling, but I was erroneously sure that it wouldn't help. It could have led to a psychiatrist who could have given me the proper medication.

CHAPTER 14

MANIC DELUSIONS OF LAW ENFORCEMENT

It was December 1979. I gradually became manic. This manic episode in the winter of 1979–1980 was similar to the one I described in the first chapter of this book and took place in the spring of 1981. During both manic episodes, I had the delusion that I was a CIA/FBI agent. According to my rough estimate, up to one-fourth of all American type-one manic depressives get the secret agent delusion. Roughly half think they are Jesus Christ, God, or the Virgin Mary. Other common delusions of grandeur include the thought that you are the reincarnation of Beatle John Lennon, a big business tycoon, or a great rap artist. One woman thought that she was the reincarnation of Noah.

When I got home after dropping out of college, I started looking for jobs in the want ads. I answered an ad to be a cab driver and got the job. I remember they checked to see if I was a criminal before they hired me. I drove a cab for two weeks until it was clear that I was hardly making any money. I kept getting lost. I was too distracted with my manic thoughts of trying to save the world from crime.

I gradually became a manic fanatic at fighting crime. I was going to the library to look up the Washington State Criminal Statutes. I thought the law that restricted cops from using their guns in situations where other people can use guns was unconstitutional. I, ridiculously, felt it was unequal protection and therefore against the Fourteenth Amendment. The cops were being discriminated against. The way I talked about— how I was going to get that law declared unconstitutional—made my dad and my brother, Rick, think I was crazy.

I heard of a drug dealer on Mercer Island who also threatened people with knives and took sexual advantage of women when they were unconscious. Consistent with my reckless, dangerous, crime-fighting urges, I told the cops I'd volunteer for an undercover drug buy. The Mercer Island police force needs the help of citizens, so they liked the idea. I went to the dealer's house with money with the serial numbers recorded to buy drugs, but he wouldn't sell any to me because he had almost been caught a couple of days earlier, and he didn't know me.

Incidentally, I should note that I've never used illegal drugs, and I've never been drunk. I believed my teachers, coaches, parents, and the cops when they said that drugs and alcohol were not the solution to life's problems.

During this manic time, I often said stuff at our dinner table—loudly. For example, I would say: "The whole Washington State Legislature has violated their oath of office! They've stopped cops from using their guns when other people can! They have violated the Fourteenth Amendment! All of the legislators should be removed from office!"

My dad started to suggest I get a shrink to get this "thing" taken care of. I didn't know what "thing" he was talking about. I wouldn't talk to him, which to me was normal, but to him wasn't. My mom was in the hospital for being manic at that time. She had been opening up all the windows in the house even though it was winter, and she had been trying to wheel herself in her wheelchair down the icy road with one hand and one foot to get to Temple Moses.

Dad said, "Mom's doctor wants you to come into the hospital, just to get started on some *medication,* to get this thing cleared up. These things can be genetic."

I had no idea of what my dad was talking about when he said, "This thing that needs taking care of." I thought it was perfectly reasonable to think that I could impeach the whole legislature. When he told me about this plan of putting me in the hospital, we were behind a closed bedroom door or in the car when nobody else was around. I thought this was just a form of abuse he was trying to keep secret. I thought he was trying to put me on mind-altering drugs to control me.

In order to get away from my dad in general, I was going to move into my grandfather's old duplex. My grandfather was in a nursing home for a while, and then he moved in with my dad. My grandpa's place was very run-down and I was going to fix it up—or so I said.

When my dad was talking to me about my "thing," he would alternate between extreme anger and telling me how much he loved me.

Once, when we were alone in his car, driving to go visit my grandfather at the nursing home, my dad said, "I'm your best friend. I'm the one who will go through thick and thin with you."

"Dad, would you just drive?"

Furiously, my dad screamed, pulling the car over. "Now listen, you! You better listen to me. You are sick! You are out of your mind! I'm helping you with a problem! Nobody else is ever going to help you as much as me!"

"Dad, you better drive, or I'll get out and hitchhike."

Then he started driving again but kept up his lecture.

When talking about my mother, he found great amusement in the idea that if she *could* talk, what she *would* say would be irrational.

About me, he said, "We'll put you in the hospital, and then you won't be mad at me. You'll be back to your old self!"

He was smiling as he said this. He said this with great contentment and enthusiasm.

Finally, one day, he threatened to have me taken out of our house in a straitjacket. Then I moved out into my grandpa's house.

I tried to get more involved in fighting crime and giving the police more power. Even though the American Civil Liberties Union usually tries to restrict police power, I tried to get them interested in expanding police power. I felt the cops were being persecuted. The American Civil Liberties Union said that there has to be a victim of the law concerning unjust use of guns by police before a suit can be filed. There would have to be a case where a cop was convicted of using his gun at the wrong time. So, a lawsuit was out. I instead decided to write a book accusing the Washington State Legislature of violating their oath of office. They are sworn to uphold the constitution, and I felt the law about when police can shoot was unconstitutional. *It didn't let the police use their guns often enough*, was my ridiculous, outlandish, manic thought.

I drove down to the University of Puget Sound and told my friends about my plans for a book. The book would say that police are a persecuted minority. My friends' reactions seemed favorable the first time I went down there.

My friends at home were beginning to think I was going crazy because I was so obsessed with fighting crime.

I had read some statistics in the paper about how much time people served in prison for various serious crimes. The amount of time was surprisingly short. The average penalty for kidnapping when the person was returned unharmed was about eight months in jail. To spend more than a year in jail, a burglar of businesses had to be convicted four times. The average time served for murder was about six years. The reason for these short times served is that there is not enough prison space. The state and federal governments choose not to spend money on keeping criminals locked up, so they let them go.

I decided I could save the world from crime by convincing all the state legislatures and Congress to build more prison space and keep it full. I would do this same kind of thinking again during my manic episode in 1981, as I described in chapter 1. The parole boards were really just rationing out the available prison space; that's why they let people go. They weren't letting people go who had been reformed or who had been punished enough. They were just too cheap to keep them locked up longer; that was my ridiculous, outlandish, manic thought.

I started calling up state officials telling them they were too easy on criminals. I called state prison guards, probation officers, prosecutors, legislators, and I also called Brett Pritchard, the congressman's son, a few times. Then I started driving to Olympia to talk to state legislators. I told them we should build more prisons to fight crime. I also told them a lot of other right-wing stuff, like "We should balance the federal budget." I thought I seemed sane because people *did* talk to me a bit.

I decided the best thing to do to save the world from crime was to run for state legislator as a Libertarian from the Tacoma area. It was 1980, so it was an election year. I thought I might as well also declare my candidacy for President of the United States in 1996. I knew you had to be thirty-five to be President, and 1996 would be the first election when I'd be thirty-five. I would run on the Libertarian ticket. The Libertarians believe government should maintain law and order but should not be involved in anything else. Some Libertarians therefore believe that the government-run currency system is wrong. For one thing, it's run by the government. For another thing, it's not based on the gold system. The previous summer, I had read a Libertarian book, and I was trying to adhere to its principles. I felt the government was focusing too much on other things and not enough on crime control.

I had the delusion that I could make a lot of money on the stock market by investing in companies that would be involved in the building of prisons—after I convinced the country to build more prisons. I bought a small amount of stock in Kaiser Cement, Fluor Construction, and Caterpillar Tractor. I thought companies like this would be involved in the construction of new prisons.

I went down to the University of Puget Sound and stayed for a day or two with my friend Randy Harold. I told all my friends from my dorm floor freshman year and others about my plans to save the world from crime. At first I think they listened, but later they thought I was crazy.

I was under the impression that the head of the criminal justice committee of the legislature was going to let me speak at a hearing of the committee. I started to get some paranoid thoughts (unrealistically fearful thoughts).

I remember saying to one of my friends, "Those legislators are going to want to shoot me after I get done speaking to them because I'm going to make them look so bad."

He said, "They won't shoot you. They just will disagree with you."

I said angrily and sarcastically, "No, it can't happen here. It can't happen here!"

I also had paranoia. I thought I was about to be rich and famous but that someone would try to steal my stocks. So, I split them into two groups and put them in two separate safety deposit boxes in two different banks.

Another thing I did that was out of the ordinary was to go to my high school biology teacher during a class and ask him for one of the fingerprick things I knew he had. We had used them for blood typing. I was going to use it to prick my finger during my speech to the criminal justice committee to dramatize crime victims. I thought the blood would be a good dramatic touch. I'm sure he was somewhat annoyed, but he gave me a couple of them.

I also had come up with the statistic for my speech that one year's worth of Washington State's crime victims would fill the King Dome stadium more than four times.

About this time, my Mercer Island friends—Stan Gold, Dave Frish, and Tom Spano—arranged a meeting with me where they tried to convince me to see a psychiatrist. They didn't like my grandiose delusion that I could save the world from crime.

Stan asked, "What's your occupation?"

I said, "I am an author and a politician."

Stan said, "You're not an author or a politician."

"I am, too."

"Why did you flunk your courses?"

"The economics they teach is garbage. It is not based on the gold standard."

"You flunked all your courses, not just economics. The old Bill Hannon would have gotten straight As."

"I had more important things to worry about."

They pointed out that I had a history of psychiatric illness.

I said, "There was never anything wrong with me in Israel, and I should sue whoever tarnished my reputation by saying there was."

The argument we had went on for about fifteen minutes before I told them to get lost, and I left.

I even took a couple of steps toward trying to gather evidence for the lawsuit against the people who had said I was crazy in Israel.

My dad was also trying to get me to see a psychiatrist. He said he would pay me to go to one. He would pay the bill, and he would also pay me. I went once, and I told the doctor that my dad wanted me to be committed to a psychiatric ward because I wouldn't talk to him in light of his attitude toward my dating. When I told the doctor that my dad was paying me to come see him, he picked up the phone to call my dad, but I wouldn't give him the number. I told him he did not have permission to talk to my father. I thought that if he heard my dad's side of the story, I'd have to come back several more times to convince the doctor of my side of the story. The doctor told me to come back another time, but I never did.

My delusions got worse. I started seeing all sorts of popular culture as having hidden meanings for a peaceful Libertarian revolution where the government cares about law and order and not about much else. I also thought we should convert to a monetary system based on gold. I thought that the movie *The Wizard of Oz* really meant "the wizard of ounce," ounces being ounces of gold. I felt that the yellow brick road that we are supposed to follow in the movie actually was made of bricks of gold. The author had been saying we should be on the gold standard, which was my opinion. Actually, though, others have interpreted this movie this way, but I thought it was a big deal. There were a bunch of other movies that I felt had hidden meanings. I can't remember them all. One was *The Rocky Horror Picture Show*. I felt that the song "Let's Do the Time Warp Again" meant let's go back to the gold standard and let's cut back the huge increase in government spending that started with President Roosevelt's New Deal.

The movie *The Sound of Music* confirmed to me that the hunt for liberty in the United States must include listening to popular music. *The Sound of Music* was a musical about people seeking freedom, so I started playing all my music, looking for more clues about freedom. An example of music that had secret coded meanings to me was Steely Dan's song "Josie," which to me sounded like "Georgie." Georgie was George Washington. I thought Steely Dan was saying that we had to get back to the principles that our country was based on. These were more Libertarian than Democratic or Republican, I felt.

Another song that became my anthem was Led Zeppelin's "Stairway to Heaven." I had interpretations for this whole song. The words all pointed to the need for a peaceful Libertarian revolution. The words, "If there's a bustle in your hedgerow, don't be alarmed now, it's just a spring clean for the May-Queen," were, I felt, talking about a rape. The words, "There walks a lady we all know, who shines white light and wants to show," were referring to the Statue of Liberty.

I had my record albums strewn all over my living room floor because I changed records so often, trying to find all the secret meanings in the words of the music. I didn't have time to put them back in their jackets.

The next thing I did was write some letters to some University of Puget Sound professors. I hand-delivered the letters. The purpose of the letters was to convert the professors to crime fighters and Libertarians. Some of the letters were misinterpreted as threats. They were pretty incoherent because I was manic and there were references to violence that they did not understand. I was trying to be clever, profound, clear, helpful, famous, and noteworthy, all at the same time. *It didn't work.* Here is one of them to Professor Cable, a math professor. The change in his name to "Capable" was on purpose then.

Feb. 12, 1980

Dear Mr. Capable,

I wish you were more capable of seeing the truth in the fact that no matter how well the flood gates are engineered, a few well-placed sticks of dynamite ruin the whole Deal. It could spell the end of an ERA. If you don't

remember that computers are just big abacuses and that we use the Arabic numeral system, you should resign.
Sincerely,

Bill Hannon

P.S. I think that before this decade is out, we should set free our notion the goal of even having an abortion. This means young, old, males, females, and return the fetus safely to the womb.

What I meant by dynamite ruining "the whole Deal" was that the penalty for vandalism is so small that you could blow up a dam and probably get only thirty days in jail for it. I capitalized Deal to refer to the New Deal, which spent government money on things other than law enforcement, like dams, many of which we don't need and are bad for the environment. I capitalized "ERA" because then it means Equal Rights Amendment. The Libertarian book I read was against the ERA. The ERA was controversial because people thought it might put women in combat.

The part about the Arabic numeral system was to tell Professor Cable, who was Jewish, to quit being so concerned about Arabs and to start being more concerned with crime at home.

The bit about abortions was me trying to sound like President Kennedy, our first Catholic president. The "before this decade is out" was also my trying to sound like Kennedy, when he was speaking of when we should send a man to the moon. I thought we should spend our money on law enforcement, so we could have peace on earth, instead of worrying about what's on the moon.

The letter looked incoherent and like a threat to this math professor who I never had for a class. The part about the "dynamite" scared him, and he called the police.

I gave out about eight or ten letters to professors. I hand-delivered the letters to these professors at their houses. I did this because I thought my message was so important, and hand-delivering them added a personal touch. I didn't realize until later that they found that to be alarming. Not all of the letters caused alarm, but a few more of them did. My wording was so confusing that people got the exact opposite meaning.

About this same time, I was also giving out my interpretation of the song, "Stairway to Heaven" as campaign literature to several people I knew on campus, including Brett Pritchard and my old camp counselor who went to school there. On the top of the interpretation of the song were the words "Bill Hannon for Legislator in 1980, for President in 1996 and again in 2000."

I just walked in and handed it to them.

Then I said, "I got to go."

I'm sure now they thought I was crazy.

I had just gotten new locks put on my part of the duplex. I figured that too many people had the keys to it. It was just in time, I found out, because my dad felt that as the landlord—and as my father—he had the right to come in at any time. On the thirteenth, the Tacoma police called his house and asked to speak to me. I wasn't there, so they talked to my dad. They told him I was wanted for creating a public nuisance, for writing threatening letters. My dad went to the county courthouse and got a commitment petition. Then he came to my door with a county social worker and tried to get in. I wouldn't let them in the door and threatened to have them arrested for trespassing. They threatened to have me forcibly committed. I didn't know that the cops wanted to talk to me until much later that evening. Later, I drove down to the University of Puget Sound in Tacoma again.

Then I went and saw Randy Harold, one of my friends from freshman year. I told him what was happening and he sounded annoyed and said, "You can't stay here forever."

I went and visited with my friend Gary Cunningham and talked with him for a while. I told him that Tacoma was the last bastion of civilization left on earth. At the time, I didn't know that the police wanted to arrest me for creating a public nuisance.

After talking to Gary, I took a walk across campus to go visit some other friends, and then campus security and a Tacoma police officer came up to me and said I had to come with them. They said the Dean of Students, Harry Arvidson, wanted to talk to me. So, I went with them, and I had no idea what it was about. We went to the Dean's office.

Mr. Arvidson asked, "Did you send threatening letters to several professors?"

I said, "No."

He asked, "Is this your handwriting?"

"Yes, but they're not threatening."

Then the cop asked, "Well, what are they supposed to think when they get a letter like that?"

"Just what it says."

The cop said, "Well, right now I've got a warrant to take you to jail and charge you with creating a public nuisance. We would, but in reading these letters, Dean Arvidson thinks you may be having some kind of psychological problem."

I said, "No, I'm fine."

The cop said, "Maybe you're using some kind of drugs."

"I've never."

Dean Arvidson said, "Well, right now I can offer you the choice of undergoing an overnight psychiatric evaluation at a hospital and doing what they say or getting arrested for creating a public nuisance."

"Well, can't I just pay a fine or something?"

The cop said, "No. You have to go to jail."

Arvidson said, "We thought this had something to do with Vice President Mondale's speech tomorrow."

"Why? What is Mondale saying tomorrow?"

Arvidson said, "We don't know what he's going to say. He's giving a speech here in Tacoma at Pacific Lutheran University tomorrow. Did you know that?"

I said, "No." That was the truth.

The cop asked, "Do your letters have something to do with that?"

"No. My letters were trying to convert the professors to my way of thinking."

I then went on about my plan for the economy that included a massive barter system with Tacoma as one of the centers. My plan seemed so farfetched that it was clear to Arvidson that I was crazy. He started crying.

Eventually he got himself together and then he asked, "Do you want to undergo a psychiatric evaluation?"

Thinking it would look bad for a crime fighter like myself to be arrested and thinking that the psychiatrist would find that I was okay, I said, "Yes, I'll get the psychiatric evaluation."

The cop walked with me out to the car in which Arvidson would drive me to the hospital. The cop and I waited in the car for Arvidson.

While we were in the car, the cop said, "This is a drag, Mondale coming to town. I have to escort some protesters who will be protesting him."

I said, "Oh, really," in a bored tone.

Arvidson came to the car and the cop got out. Then Arvidson drove me to Beasley Hospital in Tacoma. I then went to admitting. They had me turn over my wallet and keys to them for safekeeping. I remember saying that if they lost my safe deposit box keys, I would end up owning the hospital from a lawsuit.

On the admitting form that a nurse read to me they already had listed my diagnosis: manic depressive. I had never heard the term "manic depressive" before. I wrote on the form that Dr. Grisso, who had written that I was manic depressive, should lose his license for calling me manic depressive without even seeing me.

As I went into the locked psychiatric unit, I remember asking the aides who greeted me if there were any criminals on the ward.

They said, "No. We don't let them on this ward."

Then they showed me which room would be mine, and a nurse said they would start me on the mood leveler lithium. I started laughing because I knew lithium was an element on the periodic table of chemistry. I wondered if it was like helium, which is supposed to make you talk funny. It just didn't sound like a drug. I had never heard of it as a drug before. It sounded like a joke. The nurse thought my laughter was inappropriate. I refused the drug. After all, I don't do drugs—especially since I felt there was nothing wrong with me.

I went to bed that night, but I didn't sleep. Instead I looked at the spots of light on the wall projected through the windows from the streetlights, and I tried to figure out what they meant. In the morning, I met with Dr. Grisso for the first time. I told an aide to come with me as a witness.

I yelled at Dr. Grisso, "What if I hadn't scored in the 99th percentile on my verbal SATs and couldn't read that you had diagnosed me manic depressive without even seeing me?"

I forget what he said, but I told him he should lose his medical license for diagnosing me without seeing me. The whole session was mostly me yelling at him.

Later I started thinking that I was actually put in the psychiatric ward to undergo the psychological screening necessary to become a CIA/FBI agent. I decided that the Secret Service had done a background investigation on me after they heard about my "threatening" letters around the time of Mondale's visit. I decided that they discovered I was so clean that I was qualified to be an FBI agent. Plus, I figured, they knew the true meanings of my letters, so they understood I had some good ideas about stopping crime. I thought I was in training to become an FBI/CIA agent.

The nurses' notes I obtained from Beasley Hospital to help write this book say that on February 14, I got served with papers intended to tell me of my seventy-two-hour hold by the court.

I didn't read the papers. The only thing the staff said to me was, "You are on a hold."

I didn't know what that meant. I thought of the Beatles song lyrics, "You really got a *hold* on me." And I thought of a girl I went out with once at UPS.

The staff didn't say the words, "court," or "hearing."

To be held in a hospital against your will in Washington, you have to be deemed a danger to yourself or others. I was being held three days, pending the outcome of a hearing. I needed the treatment, but I didn't know it. I was a danger because of my driving 85 miles per hour, in a 55 mile per hour zone, or through other accidental means. I had also been going outside barefoot, even though it was winter. My mind was so preoccupied with manic thoughts of saving the world that I neglected all else, like safe driving and dressing for the weather. Sometimes they take just a little evidence as qualifying you as a danger to yourself or others, and you get committed and you get well. Other times the court fails to commit people who need it. Then the people often end up in a severe car accident if they are manic, or they can kill themselves deliberately if they are depressed.

The nurse report says my speech was rapid with occasional inappropriate laughter. Also, I was "guarded" in my responses to questions. This guardedness, I remember, was because I didn't know who on the ward to trust. I didn't know who was an FBI/CIA agent and who was not. I didn't know who had security clearance and who did not. I thought that some people on the floor really were regular patients and nurses, and I thought others were FBI/CIA. The civilian staff, I thought, misinterpreted a lot of my CIA-directed speech as crazy thinking. There was no point talking to them.

On February 15, I decided that there must be some codes I had to think of to be a CIA agent. There was a T-shirt that a friend of mine at the University of Puget Sound had that looked like it said something in Hebrew if you looked at it right side up, but if you looked at it upside down it said, "Go Fuck Yourself," in English. I thought this could be a code phrase.

Every few hours that I was in the hospital, a nurse would offer me medication, and I would refuse. I would refuse because I thought there was nothing wrong with me.

Sometimes they would say, "You'll feel better if you take it."

This was ridiculous because I felt fine. Manic people almost always feel fine. Unlike when I was depressed, I finally had a sense of purpose. I was CIA/FBI in training! I was excited. The nurses should have known that I felt fine. This was in spite of the fact that I hadn't slept at all since being admitted.

The nurses eventually convinced me to accept some medication by telling me, "You haven't been sleeping. These will help you sleep."

I knew a person could go insane from not sleeping, so I took the medication on two of those nights. I slept a few hours those two nights. Unfortunately, the nurses did not catch on and repeat the fact that the drugs would help me sleep. Nor was any nurse willing to stick her neck out and say that if I took the medication, I'd get out of the hospital sooner. It was really very ineffective nursing practice. I wanted to get out of the hospital, so I could be free to do what I wanted.

Nights when I was not on medication, I didn't sleep. The whole eight days that I was in Beasley Hospital, I only slept on two nights. I would go to bed on the other nights, but I would not sleep. Instead I would look at what the streetlights from across the street were projecting onto the walls of my room. I thought the CIA was actually doing the projecting, and the shadows and the lights had a secret meaning that I was supposed to pick up. It was eerie but a great adventure.

Another bizarre thing I did for a while in the hospital was, I wouldn't eat the food from the tray for me if the handwriting spelling my name was a little off. I told the staff that there were dangerous chemicals in the food. The real reason I wouldn't eat was because I thought the handwriting being a little off was a message to show that everything about my identity must be exact. I thought that whoever on the hospital staff was CIA would know that I got the message if I didn't eat. Instead, I ate some food from the refrigerator that was in the lounge of the ward.

To get my identity straight, which was what the food thing was all about, I figured they had taken hair samples off the electric razor I had borrowed from the staff. I consented also to a blood test. I thought the blood test would help to identify me also.

The 1980 Winter Olympics were on television, and Eric Heiden kept winning gold medals in speed skating. I thought, though, that the whole thing was staged and had been put on the television in the ward by the CIA. I thought it was supposed to be a message to me that I could win gold medals like the Congressional Medal of Honor, or the

Presidential Medal of Honor if I did succeed in drastically lowering the crime rate by getting more prisons built and keeping them full.

I kept requesting to leave both orally and in writing. I wanted to leave so I could be free to do what I wanted. I could still give my anti-crime speech to the legislature, even if I wasn't a CIA agent. The nurses told me there was a hold on me. They never explained that it was a court ordered hold, and a judge would decide at a hearing if I could go. They also didn't explain that if I did get committed, they would get six orderlies to tie me to a bed and give me shots. They wrote in my records, that I have now obtained, that my speech was rapid and incoherent. I'm sure it was. After all, I was speaking in a code that only the CIA was supposed to understand.

In spite of all this, I felt good. Being manic is like being in an energetic, happy mood.

Another delusion I had about the CIA was that my Uncle Mike Felber, who had died about a year earlier, actually hadn't died; I believed he had just gone undercover as a CIA agent. Also, I thought another uncle, Adam, who had died before I was born, must be deep undercover in U.S. Army Intelligence. I remember telling all these things to my cousin Laura Felber over the phone. She said it couldn't be true, because she saw her father's body and had seen pictures of Uncle Adam very sick. I'm sure talking to me was a very weird experience for her.

I had paranoia about the drugs Dr. Grisso wanted to give to me. He wanted to give me antipsychotic Haldol, which I interpreted as "Hell Doll." I figured the drug would turn me into a Hell Doll, which means I'd be doing the devil's work.

For exercise, and to kill time in the ward, I would walk the full length of the ward, back and forth, for hours. I would often flex my hands alternately like I was swimming freestyle. I felt good. The walks on the full length of the ward were every day I was in that hospital, except the two days that I took medication. The two days I took medication, my speech and motor activity were slowed down.

My mood and outlook were great. I was happy. Not only was I making the swimming motions with my hands but also I was thinking about fun times at camp and in high school, times when I was happy. I had finally been lifted out of depression and it felt great. It was very hard to convince me that there was something wrong. I thought about touch football games at my grade school playground when we had been in junior high. The athletic prowess, the toughness, the cleverness. I thought about the strategy and tactics needed to win skills competitions in Boy Scouts. I thought about the socializing during JTG overnight conclaves when I had been in senior high. I felt the thrill of doing well on tough tests in high school. I thought my studying had paid off because now I was a CIA agent in training. I now considered myself equal to my poker buddies. I had not felt equal to them since high school. They were still undergrads, and I was a CIA agent in training!

I was writing a lot of notes to be put in my chart while I was in the hospital. They were supposed to have secret meanings for those on the staff who were CIA agents. Also, I composed some letters to friends and sent a few. Here is an example. This was part of a letter dated February 17 to Stan Gold, but I never sent it:

… I would like to get out of here soon, though, who do you think I am? Alexander Soldie Nitze type? May bee I will put out the white cross = amphetamines for those who live and graves for those who die. Let's stay behind door number one. What've we got? We got a lot, we've got a team that's red hot. Sizzlae. If you go shadow dancing, Do it Right! No need to blitzkreig the combat zone type environment. War is not healthy for children or other human beings. Nation shall not lift up sword against nation, nor shall people fail to burn their draft cards. I heard when the old coach at Mercer initiated new members, they would get their head dunked in a toilet, and I love my hair. I'll keep it and wash it whenever and however I feel like it. I don't need Brett either. And I want my money …

Obviously, I was jumping from topic to topic with no apparent connection. In my mind, somehow, there was a connection, but it was not apparent to the reader. The nurses took it as evidence that I was manic. This symptom is called "flight of ideas."

On February 20, two county deputies told me they were taking me to a hearing. I wasn't sure what that meant. They told me to sit in the back of their squad car. I figured they were fellow law enforcement types, and I outranked them. I figured they wanted to help me save the world from crime. When we got to a courthouse, they walked me into the building for the hearing. It was intended to determine if I should be legally committed, which meant being forced to stay in the hospital and forced to take medication.

When I got there, the judge asked me, "Do you know why you're in the hospital?"

I said, "Yeah, some people think I'm crazy, *but I'm fine*. I want a *second opinion*. I want to switch to Dr. Kelly. He is the doctor I had in the summer of 1977 after my trip to Israel."

I thought that the fact that it was a CIA/FBI training base had to be kept secret, but Dr. Kelly would probably know both that it was an FBI/CIA training base and that it had to be kept secret. (Dr. Kelly had never really said to me that I was sick.)

The judge granted my request for a second opinion, so on February 22, I was driven to Helgerson Hospital where Dr. Kelly worked.

When I saw Dr. Kelly, I said, "Dr. Kelly, Get me out of here. I'm sure you can see I'm fine. And I should probably sue the people involved in putting me in the hospital in Israel because they mistakenly thought I was crazy, and now this inaccurate thought that I was sick before, is being used against me."

To my surprise, Dr. Kelly said, "I've read your chart, and I believe you're sick."

I asked, "What's wrong with me?"

He said, "You're manic."

"What does that mean?"

"That's the opposite of depressed."

"Well, the opposite of depressed is happy, so I'm in here because I'm happy?"

"Well, you need treatment, Bill. I'm going to put you on some medication."

That was the end of my session with Dr. Kelly for that day. I left with the impression that he was insane because he had me in the hospital to treat happiness. I had never heard the word "manic" before this manic episode.

Dr. Kelly decided I had to stay in the hospital. He was competent for not letting me go, but if he or Dr. Grisso had been better, they would have told me, "You will get out of the hospital in *three* weeks, at the latest, if you take the medication."

They didn't tell me that, so it took *six* weeks.

It *could* have been only three weeks if they would have explained that being committed meant being tied down to your bed and having the drugs injected, while taking the drugs by mouth meant getting out in three weeks without getting tied to your bed.

I did feel happy. People generally feel great when they are manic. Being happy reminded me of my days at Camp Okransky when I was age seventeen, in 1976. Feeling good like I did at camp reminded me of Joel Stein, so I called him. I told him about my main plan to get rich on the stock market by buying stocks in construction companies that build prisons, after convincing the nation's lawmakers to build more prisons. I also told him that the Secret Service was listening to the phone call. I felt they were still doing a background check on me so that they would know whether I qualified as an FBI/CIA agent.

I read now in my medical records that Joel called the nurses station to ask what the deal was with me after I called him. I hadn't seen him in three years.

The nurses' notes I got when I started to write this book say the first several days I was at Helgerson Hospital, I was "very guarded in conversation with the nurses."

I think now, that I was "guarded" in conversation with them because I thought I was on a top-secret mission.

However, after a while, I warmed up to the nurses, and I discussed some of the notes I had written to be put on my chart, but I still kept some notes secret.

One nurse asked, "What do you need?"

I told her, "I need a lot of police for security when I give my speech because a lot of criminals won't like what I will be saying."

All this while, both at Beasley Hospital, and Helgerson Hospital, I was refusing medication, and sleeping very little if at all. I was spending my time writing bizarre notes to be put in my chart. I knew that the nurses were having trouble understanding my notes, but I felt someone who really knew me and understood me could understand them. I felt the FBI was investigating me thoroughly enough so that they would understand the notes.

Let's get back to Dr. Kelly. Almost every day that he saw me up until March 5, he said, "If you don't take the medication, you'll be locked up."

I would say, "I'm already locked up," because I already was in a locked ward from which I could not leave.

That was his chance to say that if I got committed, they would get six orderlies to hold me down, tie me to a bed, and give me shots. He never said that. I wish he would have. The nurses never said that either. Also, neither Dr. Kelly nor the nurses ever said I'd get out in three weeks if I took the medication. I wanted to get out.

If they would have said, "You'll be tied to your bed," I probably would've taken the medication by mouth in pill form.

They all only said, "It depends what happens at your next hearing."

Finally, on March 5, I was escorted by two sheriff's deputies to my second hearing.

There, my *court appointed lawyer* who I had just met, told me what happens if you get committed. He said, "If you get committed—and I think you will be—they will get six men to strap your body to the bed and inject drugs into your body, and you won't be able to move. If you agree to take the drugs voluntarily, by mouth, you can avoid that and be free."

So, I told the judge that I would take the drugs, and I avoided being legally committed.

I was driven back to the hospital by the deputies, and I started taking the drugs. The next morning, I woke up and was very surprised. I thought, *Oops! I guess this isn't a CIA training base.* They gave me a higher dose than they had given me when I had agreed to try the meds for two days.

As I started taking the drugs, I got less hyperactive. I was on antipsychotic Haldol and mood leveler lithium. I also got the side effects of lithium. My muscles started to twitch. Any muscle I used twitched. (This is properly called muscle tremor.) Nurses earlier had said, "Lithium is a salt, not a drug."

I thought they were saying it was "assault." Now that was coming true. It was an assault on my muscles. (It doesn't cause muscle tremor in most people.)

I devoted less time to my note writing and started getting to know the other patients. There were a bunch of fourteen-year-old runaway girls, a few people in for alcoholism, and a couple general juvenile delinquent boys. There were several people in for depression. There was one accused murderer. He had apparently stabbed a woman seven times in a robbery. He was undergoing a pre-trial psychiatric evaluation. He did not belong there. He was harassing the depressives.

After a week or so of taking antipsychotic Haldol, mood leveler lithium, and side effect drug Cogentin, I was transferred to the open ward. The Cogentin was for the muscle stiffness side effect of Haldol. The open ward provided occupational therapy, group therapy, and recreational therapy.

Some of the nurses on the open ward were helpful in talking about my parents. Still, they never gave me a list of symptoms of manic depression, and they didn't talk about the symptoms directly. Their attitude was, "Well let's just get these past few months over with. Take your lithium. It can help. It helps keep you on an even keel."

They were too honest to say that lithium would definitely make me perfectly healthy. There was hesitation in their voice when they said, "It helps keep you on an even keel." From their tone, it was clear that they were not so sure.

Once I got over to the open ward, people started visiting me and saying I sounded "much better" on the phone. I also gradually realized that I had a problem and that I would need to take mood leveler lithium indefinitely. I hated lithium because of the muscle tremors, but I would put up with it for a while. I still wanted to save the country from crime, but I knew I couldn't do it easily. Finally, on March 27, 1980, I was discharged. I went back to my grandfather's duplex. Let's hear it for the medicine!

Chapter 15

Another Year of Depression and No Good Doctor

I left the hospital mostly thinking the manic depression was due to stress. I would sometimes tell people that it was the stress of my mother's stroke and what it did to my family. Dr. Kelly returned to his mute stance of failing to give information about the genetic aspect of it, the symptoms to watch for, or all the appropriate drugs.

I continued to blame my dad's behavior for all my problems. In reality, it would have been much better to change my genes than to change my father. I didn't know that then. Dr. Kelly continued to be nearly mute. If Dr. Kelly had known what he was doing, he would have told me right away that the problem was from my mom's genes. Then I could've quit blaming my dad sooner.

I went down to the University of Puget Sound to visit my friends. I told them I was okay now and wouldn't be saving the world. I remember telling Wayne, my roommate from freshman and sophomore year, that I was really upset that my muscles twitched.

I said, "I want to be the body beautiful."

He said, "You just have to live with it," or something like that.

I hung around campus for about a day, and then went back home to my grandpa's duplex on Mercer Island.

A few days later Stan Gold came over and helped me put all my musical records back in their album covers. He also urged me to keep up in doing my dishes. That was nice. I needed the encouragement.

There was a bunch of old washing machines and other junk in the basement of the duplex that needed to be taken to the junk yard. My Grandpa used to repair washing machines. So, one Saturday morning I got a group of my poker buddies to help haul the stuff upstairs to a truck and take it to a junkyard to recycle the metal. It was grueling work, but we had made a dent in the huge pile of junk. I bought my friends lunch for helping me.

Feeling like my place was set up, my next step was a career. My career plans were now to become a computer programmer. I enrolled in a private trade school for an eighteen-month course in computer programming. I promptly quit after flunking the first four tests. I had poor concentration. I had the usual "I am a loser," depressed thoughts on my mind.

An instance of poor medical practice by Dr. Kelly that year was his failure to prescribe an antidepressant medication for me, even though I made it clear that I was depressed. Antidepressants are some of the main drugs used in treating manic depression, but he never even mentioned them. I had never heard of them. Even though I always complained of symptoms of depression, he never told me it was treatable. A person can take antidepressants in addition to mood leveler lithium to combat depression when the lithium fails to prevent it. He also never gave me a list of symptoms of depression and never gave me a list of symptoms of mania. When I went to see him once a month, he would hardly say a thing. I would talk and he would just sit there and take notes. If I asked a question, I would have to ask twice to get an answer. I remember once he did say there are genetic factors in manic depression. I thought that that just applied to the manic part, not the depressed part. He didn't take my depression seriously enough to talk about it. At that point, I didn't know he was a bad doctor because I didn't know what a good doctor was. Now I do, so I know he was awful. I feel he was botching the job every time I saw him. He should have told me more about my prognosis. He should have told me more about symptoms, side effects, and medication. He should have given me literature. If he would have told me more about the genetic aspects, I would know that the problem was from within me and not environmental.

When I flunked out of the computer school, as a victim of bad medicine, I decided I wanted to go back to the University of Puget Sound.

In the meantime, I usually went to bed late, about eleven at night, after listening to Larry King or Sally Jesse Raphael on the radio. Then I would sleep late, and I wouldn't get out of bed until my mother would call on the phone. She couldn't talk, but she could dial the phone, and then say "Dee de dee" in sentences.

Then I got out of bed and talked to her.

She would always ask as best she could, "Are you awake?" I could tell by the tone of her voice.

I would always say that I was awake but still in bed, which I was. I would talk to her for a few minutes, take a shower, and then get dressed. Then I would get some breakfast. It was always cold cereal. I didn't cook much.

For activities that summer, I watched lots of television. I did go jogging with my poker friend Jack Johnson sometimes because I remember complaining about my muscle tremors to him. I jogged with his sister a few times also.

I was terribly unhappy, though. Difficulty getting out of bed is a sure sign of depression. Plus, I would never do my dishes. I would just wash one dirty one from the dirty dish pile when I needed a clean one. Then, when I was through with that one, I'd put it back on the dirty dish pile. I had no energy. I still viewed the world as a crummy place because of all the crime. It still looked like something desperately had to be done to save the world. My outlook was not rosy. It was very dreary.

This whole year, my dad would invite me over to his house for Friday night Sabbath dinner. It was okay. It was a good chance to see my mom and my two younger brothers.

My dad's financial support saved me from being homeless. He gave me money every month, without which I may have ended up as just another mentally ill street person. I was very lucky that he was willing and able to give me money. During this time and during many future years, he gave me money for medicine, doctors, rent, food, tuition, and cars. He was really very helpful. His generosity made my eventual recovery possible. Thousands of manic depressives are homeless and never recover. My dad was making my life livable.

Being depressed, I sat or lay around a lot, sometimes listening to music, sometimes not. I listened to a lot of Rolling Stones' music as well as lots of other rock and roll. I would often listen to the same song or same side of a record over and over. Spending so much time doing nothing, just listening to music, or watching television was clearly a symptom of depression. I would see Dr. Kelly once in a while, and he would say nothing. I was on mood leveler lithium (at blood level 1.0) and side effect drug Cogentin (1 mg per day), and I was miserable. The blood level is the measure of how much drug is in your bloodstream. They take a test tube full of blood and test for the drug. The level in your blood tells you how to adjust the dosage. I was on a full dose of lithium, but the Cogentin was a mistake. Cogentin is for stopping the muscle stiffness and restlessness side effect of antipsychotics. It did nothing for the tremors of lithium. Therefore, Dr. Kelly should not have prescribed it. Cogentin may have given some side effects of its own.

My mother was in a nursing home off and on during this year, mainly for depression. She wouldn't eat, she was so depressed, and she wouldn't do anything. My dad couldn't take care of her, so she had to go into a nursing home. I went to visit her, and she was glad to see me, but she still didn't eat. I was told they couldn't give her medication that would help because of her heart condition.

During winter quarter, I had the chance to go back to University of Puget Sound, but I stayed in Seattle and went to the University of Washington, like I had fall quarter. I went to UW because they had a program with the state legislature in Olympia where a student could go to the Capitol and assist state legislators for a few days a week. In turn, the student would learn about the legislative process. There was also a one-hour-a-week class to go along with the internship. I had a car, so I could make the sixty-mile trip to Olympia.

I went to the Capitol in Olympia and filled out an application. I said I wanted to work for a Republican. I wanted someone who was tough on crime and in favor of a free-market economy. A few days later, I called back, and they said they had a legislator who was willing to interview me. His name was Andy Denslow. I had an interview with him. I told him I was a political science major, and I was having trouble getting excited about school, but I thought that some actual hands-on political experience would help get me excited about school. I believed that to a degree. I thought a stimulating environment was the key to cheering me up. Representative Denslow agreed to have me work with him for a few days a week. He was a Born-Again-Christian and a big supporter of Ronald Reagan.

So, I started driving down to Olympia three mornings a week. I observed committee meetings, talked to lobbyists, stuffed some envelopes, and answered some letters. Andy Denslow authored one criminal law that passed the legislature that year. It was a law making it a felony to flee a police officer in a motor vehicle. It was designed to help cut down on high-speed chases. We discussed other crime issues too. I decided that after the quarter was over, I would again try to lobby the legislature for tougher sentencing facilitated by building more prison space. I talked to a couple of legislators about crime while I was still working for Representative Denslow, which I wasn't supposed to do without his permission.

I wrote to the embassy of every Western European country I could think of and asked them a bunch of questions about crime in their countries. By the end of the quarter, the embassies, except for a couple, came through with a lot of information. It is sort of manic to write to embassies, although in this case I know I was still depressed and thinking that someone had to do something about the depressing crime problem.

Toward the end of the quarter, in early March 1981, my mom died. Her heart valve gave way. We had a funeral and held mourning sessions in the evenings for seven days, which is the Jewish tradition. At the funeral, I thought about how this was the end of an era, and that our family could not be put back together. A new era was beginning. The only memory that really stands out from the burial is that everyone pulled up in their cars and didn't say anything. All you heard was the car doors opening and slamming. Otherwise, there was silence. That was the sound of burial. Car doors and silence.

I thought, as one of my friends said, that my mom's death was a relief for her and for the rest of us. My mother was usually very depressed; she couldn't talk, read, or write, and she was paralyzed on one side. I hoped my dad would remarry.

I started getting more excited about fighting crime again. I started to get manic again in spite of being on medication. It was April 1981.

This April 1981 manic episode is the manic episode that I described in the first chapter of this book. It was very similar to the winter 1980 manic episode of chapter 14. This chapter 1 episode was called "KGB Bloodhounds." It was when I thought the FBI/CIA was trying to help get me elected to Congress. In the meantime, I had the delusion that I was CIA. I was down at UPS, wandering around at night. I stopped at a dorm lounge to read the secret clues in the late night Associated Press written news that scrolled up the television screen. Later, a dog was following me, and I thought it was trailing my scent for the KGB. I swam across a pond, so the dog would lose my scent. I ended up in a stranger's dorm room because I thought we were all supposed to switch rooms to confuse the KGB. I ended up in the psych ward of a hospital in April 1981, just like I did after the episode in February 1980 that I wrote about in the previous chapter. I got out again, thanks to medication. Then I had a good summer in 1981.

CHAPTER 16

THE GOOD SUMMER OF 1981

I got out of the hospital in late April 1981 and went back to my place in my grandfather's duplex. I was there a few weeks, and then Dr. Holley—whom I had switched to when I started to get manic—said I should move in with my dad because it was less stressful than living alone. I reluctantly agreed, but it worked out okay. Fortunately, my brothers, Steve and Johnny, were there, and for a while my brother, Rick. I decided I would go back to the University of Puget Sound in the fall, even though my classmates had graduated. My main reason for going back down there in the fall was that they had coed dorms, and it would be a chance for me to have a good social life and possibly fall in love. In late May, I got a job as cashier at a convenience store. It was a minimum wage job, of course, but I couldn't handle it. I couldn't learn how to work the cash registers. I quit after three days. I was still on a lot of antipsychotic medication.

Dr. Holley now had me thinking I was schizophrenic. But I asked him, "What caused my episode down on campus?"

In spite of blood tests that he ran that said I was not using illegal drugs, he said, "Oh, I just think you were smoking a little grass."

I said, "No, so what caused it?"

"Well, I think you were a little depressed about your mom's death."

"Well, not really, but wouldn't what I did be the manic part and not depressed?"

"Well, you can act strange when you are depressed, too."

"I wasn't that depressed."

"Well, a parent's death can be a big stress on someone."

I said, "Maybe I'll be okay now that I got out my feelings about my mom and what it does to my family."

I somehow had picked up the idea that suppressed feelings pop out later and are the cause of nervous breakdowns. This idea is not true for manic depression, but it is a common myth. It may be true for other things.

"I think you probably will be okay as we gradually reduce the dose of this antipsychotic Haldol in the next couple weeks," said Holley.

It was this assurance that made me think that the disease was behind me. I thought it would not bother me again unless I was under severe stress, like someone else's death. Overall, he maintained that I was schizophrenic, not manic depressive, and I would probably be fine for a long time. This somehow made sense then, but of course it does not make sense. It made sense because I temporarily felt okay. I thought that feeling would last awhile.

Given that I was fairly healthy, it was the time to ask me about the content of my delusions and to figure out what the problem in April had been. If he had determined that I was schizophrenic, he probably should have put me on antipsychotic medication; if he had determined that I was manic depressive, then he should have tried me back on mood leveler lithium or something else for manic depression. Instead, after a couple of weeks, he had me on nothing. He thought that talking to him would keep me stable. I recognize this as extremely poor medical practice now, though I didn't recognize it then. I've learned much since then. Misdiagnosis is a big error. I could have gotten better sooner with an earlier diagnosis. However, my mood was temporarily good.

In mid-June, we had our stag party for high school poker friends Jack and Jim. They were getting married to their sweethearts of several years that summer. We had dinner in a private room in a restaurant. I was feeling very good. This feeling good was random luck, but I didn't know that. We had speeches and presentations of gifts. The speeches were to be roasts of Jack and Jim. A cousin of Jack's gave a good roast of Jack. He told a lot of funny stories from when they were little.

Jim's brother roasted him. He pointed out many escapades of Jim's where Jim ended up looking stupid. This included a time when he was so drunk he couldn't stand up. "I had to help him get his contacts out and undress him so he could go to bed," said his brother.

I wished that my manic episodes were just one-nighters, yet I prided myself in knowing not to get drunk. Many manic depressives are chemically dependent, which means addicted to alcohol or street drugs. Then they have two major mental illnesses. My avoidance of drinking was partly due to school health programs saying "Your problems will still be there when the drugs or alcohol wears off."

My father, my doctors, and my swim coaches had also told me not to drink.

At the stag party, I gave the presents to Jim. I felt like I was just one of the guys. I was on equal footing with them, and I had just taken some time off school. I said, "When we used to play cards and Jim would win, we would always say, 'Will Eckhart go to college with his poker winnings?' Well, he not only went to college, he even graduated." I went on to say, "He probably paid for his condo with poker winnings, too." Then I presented him with our gift, which was a briefcase. He had graduated from the University of Washington with a degree in electrical engineering.

Dave Frish presented the gifts to Jack Johnson. Both Dave and Jack were about to start graduate school at UW in aerospace engineering. We gave him a tool set because he had just bought a car. It was such a homey, middle class, typical American gift, that I felt some reassurance that I was part of it all. I had felt out of step since 1976. I also liked the idea that people my age could get married.

Jim and Jack gave some gag gifts to the four of us who threw the party. I had always been slim and trim, but I had gained twenty-five pounds since I got out of the hospital.

So, Jim said, "To Bill, who used to always pride himself at being a good swimmer, and being in shape, who is now so fat all he can do is float. We hereby enroll him in the Orson Welles diet plan."

That got a good laugh from the group. I didn't mind.

We had about thirty-three guys there, and about twenty stayed to play poker. We gave part of each pot to Jim and Jack.

Jack's wedding was first. It was at Temple Moses and there was a dinner at a hotel afterward. His best man, who had been his roommate in college, chained up their bed in their bridal suite and put the key to the lock inside one of many balloons in the bathtub. I thought it was pretty childish. I didn't like the idea of anything interfering with someone's love life.

In early July, Jim got married. It was also at Temple Moses, and they had a dinner there. I was an usher for his wedding. It was a happy occasion. I thought my life could be happy now, also.

I took some summer courses at UW. There were two summer sessions. During the first session, I took a statistics course. I got a B in it. In the second session, I took two business courses, and I got an A and a B. With some great luck, my mood was good that summer, which is what enabled me to concentrate. My mood was the best it had been since the disease started. Being manic had brought me out of my depression. I felt like I would be okay, and my insurance was seeing Dr. Holley. Knowing about antidepressants and knowing that sleeplessness was an early warning sign of mania would have been better insurance, but Dr. Holley kept me uninformed. He said as long as I got Bs at UW, he would tell my father it was okay for me to go back to college at UPS in Tacoma.

CHAPTER 17

A SEARCH FOR A HAPPY ENVIRONMENT

Dr. Holley wrote a letter to the UPS dean that said I had recovered enough to be readmitted. Luckily, the dean agreed to let me back in, and fortunately, my dad approved and agreed to pay for my room, board, tuition and books. My dad was very generous and also gave me money for clothes and shoes, and he gave me some spare cash if I needed it for recreation, sports, concerts, dancing, my social life or dating.

Many manic depressives end up homeless, so it's a great thing that I have a father who helps me so much. At the time, though, I still blamed the illness mostly on him.

My Dad drove me back down to UPS, and the ride was pleasant.

They assigned me a nice roommate named Paul. I told him I had taken time off because of illness. I said, "Now I'm okay, but I'm still seeing a shrink."

I really thought I would be okay since I thought the problem was mostly environmental, and now with the death of my mother, my father would be under less stress. I still didn't realize the problem was mostly in my genes, because Dr. Holley had failed to tell me so. That was horrible medical practice.

Classes started, and I took art history, which I needed for distribution requirements, and a course on the political economy of capitalism. My plan was to major in economics.

Early in the quarter I went to my economics major advisor, who was also the head of the economics department, and asked him what sort of a future there was for economics majors. In other words, I asked, "Can you get a job with an economics degree?"

He tried to tell me yes, and I asked him to name what jobs people got out of last year's graduating class of economics majors. He went down the list of last year's graduates. For some of them, he named a graduate school. For some he named a specific job. For others, he just said, "Job."

I asked him, "What job?"

He said, "I don't know."

This was a bad sign. That meant he was just guessing or hoping that they had jobs. They probably didn't have jobs.

I started to think that I should major in electrical engineering. That way I'd be more likely to get a good job when I graduate. UPS didn't offer an electrical engineering degree, so I started considering transferring back to UW at Seattle where I could major in electrical engineering. I really felt optimistic. I felt that now I was okay, and now I could take on something like electrical engineering. The idea that I was healthy enough to handle the toughest undergraduate major, electrical engineering, was unrealistic, and an idea given to me by Dr. Holley. That was lousy medical practice.

That quarter at Puget Sound, I started jogging every day until I sprained my ankle playing touch football. I gradually lost weight when I was jogging. I thought I was losing weight because of the jogging. I'm sure now that the real reason I was losing weight was because I was becoming depressed again. Changes in appetite are a symptom of depression. I was eating less and was glad about that. I didn't know it was related to the other symptoms I was developing.

In the evening, I would lie on my bed trying to read my art history book or my economics books, and I would just gradually put my head down on my bed and fall asleep for a half hour at a time. This wasn't normal, because I was sleeping well at night. This was the sleep disturbance symptom of depression, which can include sleeping too much.

I was also becoming concerned about crime again. This time, though, it wasn't in a manic way; it was in a depressed way. I didn't think I could save the world from crime. I was just worried about the crime that could happen around me. I heard that there was someone being allowed back on Puget Sound campus for winter quarter. He had been kicked off for a year for breaking into people's rooms. I heard that he was also a rapist, although that was unproven. I went to the president of the university to complain about his being allowed back on campus.

He said, "Thanks for telling me. You've done the right thing.
I'll check into it."

He talked to the dean of students, who just assured him that the guy was going to be on probation.

I also wrote an anonymous letter to the editor of the Puget Sound school newspaper saying the student being allowed back was a rapist and shouldn't be let back on campus.

As the quarter progressed, my mood was getting worse, I was getting more depressed. I was driving up to see Dr. Holley in Seattle every three weeks.

Once in a while he'd say, "I've got a new drug I want you to try."

I told him, "No, I don't use drugs." I figured, as many people do, that all drugs for the mind are addictive and dangerous in other ways also.

"It'll help you sleep."

"I'm sleeping too much as it is."

"Oh, this is a fun drug, you'll like it. A lot of people like it."

"No. I don't do drugs."

"This is a lot better than the ones I had you on last spring."

"No. I don't ever want to be on drugs again."

"Well this one is different. It will help you sleep."

"I'm sleeping too much as it is."

He may have been trying to give me antidepressants, which would have been right, but he didn't tell me what they were, what they were for, or what they would do. I thought they were sleeping pills. I had never heard of antidepressants. He didn't tell me that they could cheer me up.

I thought a girlfriend was the key to being happy. Of course, this was unrealistic. What I really needed was treatment for manic depression.

As the quarter progressed, negative thoughts preoccupied me more and more. The negative thoughts interfered with normal daily activities like talking and flirting. I often ate alone. Sometimes I'd eat with Paul or with one of the guys who lived on our floor. With women, I was at a loss for words. I wasn't in a good enough mood to talk to them and I didn't know how to tell them about my illness.

The quarter ended and I got a C in economics and a D in art history. I went home to Mercer Island, not knowing I was medically depressed and not knowing there was treatment for depression that worked. I thought my problem was simply that I was just not motivated or excited by economics and that I didn't have a girlfriend.

I got a temporary job as a Christmas rush helper for United Parcel Service. I rode around with a regular driver and ran up to the houses with the packages. It paid $7.80 an hour, which was outstanding pay back then. My concentration was lousy though. I almost got hit by a car, because I didn't look both ways when crossing the street.

The whole time, I was agonizing about whether or not I should go back to Puget Sound, major in economics, and graduate in '83. The other option was to switch back again to UW and major in engineering and graduate in '84. I did a passable job as a delivery helper in spite of this dilemma preoccupying my mind. It wasn't that hard a job.

I thought if I was unhappy while majoring in economics, then economics was the problem. It didn't occur to me that there was a chronic, built-in problem with my brain chemistry. Nobody had said that yet. Not a single doctor. Nobody. I thought the problem was environmental. I thought my manic episodes that required hospitalization had been due to high stress. I didn't have insight into the chronic depressed phase.

I remember jogging with Jack Johnson in December and discussing with him the idea that I could make $26,000 a year as a first-year electrical engineer or $17,000 a year as a first-year average economics graduate. I remember even taking into account the interest on the money I would save by graduating sooner. In the end, I decided that the pay differential for engineers was overwhelming, so I decided to transfer to the UW School of Engineering. I did this even though it meant waiting until 1984 to graduate. I thought the lure of high pay would motivate me and keep my spirits, concentration, and energy up. I planned to live at home with my dad, brother Johnny, and Grandpa, and I planned to commute to UW.

CHAPTER 18

GETTING DIAGNOSED AND ASCENDING FROM THE DEPTHS OF DEPRESSION

Winter quarter 1982 started, and I had a physics class, a physics lab, and a calculus class. Things were okay for about a week. Then my depression grew worse. I started to be obsessed with guilt about the letter I had written to the UPS school newspaper saying that the guy who was being let back on campus was a rapist. They never printed the letter, but I thought enough people may have read it so that I could get sued for libel. I had not even signed the letter, but I had told one person on the newspaper staff over the phone that I wrote it. Realistically, the letter was thrown away and forgotten about, but depression is not realistic. My guilt feelings were exaggerated greatly. They preoccupied my mind so much that I couldn't pay attention in class. I couldn't study either. I did really poorly on some tests.

This entire time, Dr. Holley was prescribing nothing.

When my guilt got so bad that I wasn't getting out of bed to go to school and wasn't sleeping at night, Dr. Holley said, "Well maybe you're getting depressed again."

It was true. I was getting depressed, but when he said "again" I'm sure he meant that to mean manic, the opposite. Somehow, he confused the two, as he had confused them before. He prescribed some antipsychotic Thorazine for me, which is the treatment for mania. *It is the opposite of the treatment for depression. It drags you down!* I took the Thorazine and it made me worse. I went back to him in a week. That week I spent eighteen hours a day in bed feeling paralyzed with guilt. When the phone rang, I was afraid that it was the police wanting to question me about the crime of defamation of character.

This time, my depressive string of thoughts made me worry so intensely that I could not sleep at night. Then, I would stay in bed during the day to catch up on sleep. As before, I will show my thoughts. They went something like this:

Oh, why did I write that letter? I'm such a criminal. Here I am trying to say I'm against crime, at least I'm a good guy, and then I go and pull something like this. I'm going to get arrested for defamation of character. I am going to get sued. I'm going to get attacked by the asshole who really is a rapist, but I can't say so because the world is such an upside-down, unfair, crummy place. The innocent go to jail. The guilty go free. What a rotten place the world is. There is no hope. I shouldn't have written that letter. I am a dirtball. I'm an unusually disgusting person in a disgusting world.

I managed to make it to Dr. Holley's office.

Holley said, "Let's try lithium."

I knew I felt awful whenever I had been on the mood leveler lithium, so I asked, "Is there something besides lithium that you can give me?"

"Lithium is the drug of choice."

"Is there something besides lithium?"

"Lithium is the drug of choice."

Of course, mood leveler lithium is not the drug of choice for depression. One of the twenty antidepressants along with lithium is. So, the lithium prescription without antidepressants was a serious mistake, as was the prescription for antipsychotic Thorazine. I quit the Thorazine and started lithium.

I made it out to campus one day around then, and I ran into an old friend who I used to hang around with in junior high. His name was Carl Paige. I told him how awfully bad I was doing. Later he called me up and invited me over to his apartment to try to cheer me up. That was nice. I was still staying in bed for eighteen hours most days.

I thought of someone cheerful who could maybe cheer me up. It was Jane Eggers, who had been the resident advisor of my dorm floor sophomore year and was a psychology major. I knew she was in town. She seemed always in a good mood, so it seemed like a good idea. I called her and we made plans to have lunch. On that day, I struggled out of bed and made it there. I told her of my situation, my guilt feelings, and so on.

She said, "You can't get sued if they don't print the letter." We had a good talk and she said I could call her again.

Lunch with Jane still did not relieve my total preoccupation with the idea that I was going to be sued for libel. My dad was getting concerned at this point. The mood leveler lithium was doing nothing. The next time I went to see Dr. Holley, my dad came with me.

He said, "I want Bill to get a second opinion. I want him to see an expert on this condition he has."

Dr. Holley referred us to Dr. Teresa Haglund. She was a professor of psychiatry at the University of Washington Medical School. She occasionally saw patients herself. When we first went to see her, she talked to both of us for a while, and then she talked to my dad and me separately.

I told her, "I am spending all day, every day, lying in bed feeling guilty about the letter I wrote."

She said, "You need an antidepressant."

I had never heard the word before!

Then, Dr. Haglund ordered a dexamethasone suppression test. It tests for chemicals in your blood that change in amount when you are depressed. She said she would give me an antidepressant next time I came. She also said, after asking several questions, that I was manic depressive and that the illness was mostly genetic. I hadn't known that it was mostly genetic. I should have been told sooner, so I would have quit blaming my dad sooner. I got the genes from my mom. Dr. Haglund asked me questions about the episodes during which I had been hospitalized.

She asked, "Were you on a mission to save the world?"

I said, "Well, yes. I was going to save the world from crime."

Dr. Haglund asked, "Did you sleep? Did you have high energy?"

"I didn't sleep much. I had a lot of energy."

She went on to ask many more questions about these episodes and concluded they were manic. She was the first doctor to ask me what I was thinking and why I was doing what I was doing when I was manic. My previous doctors had relied on thirdhand or fourthhand information. Dr. Haglund then asked me when I had been depressed in the past, when the depression started, if I had felt hopeless, and many other questions about specific symptoms. She concluded that I certainly had a pattern of depression.

She said, "Well, it looks like you have a clear case of manic depression."

This definitive diagnosis of manic depression was five years late and was desperately needed. I was upset to hear that it was largely genetic because you can change your environment, but you can't change your genes. Even though it was upsetting to learn that it is genetic, I needed to know. In a way, though, I was relieved to get a definite diagnosis. At least there was a word for my disease, which meant someone somewhere must have had it before. I had never met another manic depressive in my life outside the hospital. The exception to this was my mom, but I wasn't clear about her disease, and we hadn't been able to talk about it because she couldn't talk due to her stroke. At least it was a specific disease. It meant it wasn't my fault, and I was glad there were medications designed for it.

I went back to see Dr. Holley because I had visited Dr. Haglund just for a second opinion.

When Holley asked what Dr. Haglund had said, I said, "Haglund says I need an antidepressant."

Dr. Holley said, "I'll give you an antidepressant."

So, he wrote a prescription for guilt-stopping, cheer-inducing, energy-inducing, tear-stopping, sleep-normalizing, antidepressant Asendin. I think he gave me fifty milligrams to start. That night I took some before I went to bed. I slept well for the first time in weeks, and I woke up feeling better, less guilty, and more energetic!

About the second or third day of my treatment with antidepressant Asendin, my dad had a second date with a Jewish widow named Connie Palmberg. He got home at about eleven thirty at night. I asked loudly and sarcastically, "What are you doing out this late, Dad?"

He came bursting into my room and asked loudly, "Do you feel okay?"

I yelled, "Get out of my room!" Then I went into his room.

He followed me into his room, and then he yelled, "Is it this new medication that's making you act disturbed?"

I walked back into my room and yelled, "This new medication makes me feel better! I slept well the last two nights for the first time in weeks!"

He walked back into my room, and I yelled, "Get out of my room!"

My dad yelled, "I'm going to call your doctor!" and left my room.

My dad did call Dr. Holley the next day. Then Dr. Holley's office called and said Holley wanted to see me. So, the next day I went and saw him and I asked him a lot of questions, which he didn't answer—but he did say to increase the dose to 100 mg per day. That helped even more. Now I was even less depressed. It was just in time to sign up for spring classes, so I signed up for an accounting and an economics course. Engineering was out because, of course, I had failed every class winter quarter. I got Dr. Holley to sign a form excusing me for flunking because of illness.

Meanwhile, my dad was seeing a lot of Connie Palmberg, and I was thrilled. I was very glad that now my dad had someone for companionship. I now expected him to get his companionship from Connie. Because of his relationship with Connie, he was finally in a position to see that dating is great.

For several days, I followed him around the house yelling, "Do you think I liked it when you screamed at me for dating a girl who wasn't Jewish? Do you think I enjoyed it when I had a steady girlfriend who was Jewish, and you told me to quit seeing her?

He said, "I never said that."

Ideally, I would have gotten happier sooner, so I would not have been obsessed with my dad's or my own mistakes of the past. I was seeing both Dr. Haglund and Dr. Holley that spring and summer. The problem with my treatment was that I was still on only 100 mg of antidepressant Asendin until the middle of June of 1982. I eventually learned that the best dose of Asendin for me was 400 mg. So, while I was better, I was still depressed. However, my concentration was improved enough for me to get Cs in the accounting and economics classes I took in the spring. I quit feeling guilty. I stayed in bed only eight hours. I got up and went to school.

In late May, my dad and Connie got married. At the reception,

I gave a big trophy to the couple that fixed them up. It said, "For Excellence in Matchmaking."

After that, I could say things to my dad like,

"I'm going away to do things with people. I'll be back later."

He almost never protested.

The antidepressant Asendin that I was now on gave me new life. I felt like I had emerged from a cocoon to discover that the world was still there. The world had gone on without me but was waiting for me to return to it. I felt I could understand people better and do more. Just walking around campus to my classes felt like a privilege and a joy. I felt so good on 300 mg of Asendin toward the end of the summer that it reminded me of the summer of 1976. (Dr. Haglund had eventually increased the dosage.)

I was reminded of people I had known at Camp Okronsky. Those were fun times. I wrote Joel Stein and told him that a new day had dawned in my life.

I would often make hand-flexing motions like I was swimming without even consciously thinking about swimming at first. This was because I swam when I was happy and the feeling I had now was fairly happy, so it reminded me of swimming in high school. Thanks to antidepressant Asendin, I had energy and started jogging to get ready for an Outward Bound backpacking trip. I felt adventurous. I went on the backpacking trip and had a good time. I functioned well enough. I took antidepressant Asendin during the backpacking trip, but decided not to tell the other people on the trip what it was for. I functioned well enough so that it wasn't an issue. This was way better than lying in bed eighteen hours a day feeling guilty over nothing. Asendin had saved me!

About a week later, Dr. Haglund made a stupid recommendation. "Try going off your antidepressant Asendin," she suggested.

This was bad advice because when I went off it, I immediately got depressed again. She should have told me to go back on it right away if I got depressed again. I started obsessing about Melanie Carson, my high school classmate whom I had gotten to know on the senior class trip to Jamaica. I wished she would be mine, so she could cheer me up. This is the same as the depressive, obsessive wishing that I did in 1977, but this was 1982. Also, when a person goes off antidepressant Asendin, he or she suddenly feels more interested in romance, in spite of being depressed. Asendin causes erectile dysfunction in most men who use it. Asendin is one of the worst antidepressants as far as one's love life is concerned. While off Asendin, all I could do was think about Melanie. I called her twice in one day and left messages. She didn't return the calls.

After a few days. I went back on antidepressant Asendin because I was having concentration difficulties in class. In spite of the side effects, Asendin was good because it could make my mind work. It stopped me from always thinking about crying. It gave me some energy, gave me some concentration, and it stopped the topic of suicide from crossing my mind. This was as long as I was on at least 300 mg of it.

In early August, Mercer Island High Class of 1977 had our five-year reunion. I went and thought it was reasonably interesting and enjoyable. I did feel bad that at this point I was neither a college graduate nor married. I talked to some people I knew and caught up on what they were doing. The reunion was interesting, but I wished people had known that I had been through the twilight zone and was not quite back. I wanted some sympathy. On the other hand, I didn't want people to know all the crazy things I'd done. I wanted to fit in like I had in high school. I didn't talk to too many people at length, but I did tell people I had manic depression.

Elsewhere in my small social life, my cousin Laura Felber convinced me to join the Seattle Area Jewish Dating Service.

I went out with a couple of women from the dating service once each, and one woman about three times, but nothing romantic ever happened. I had been on enough Asendin throughout the summer that I was able, for the first time in a long time, to get a full quarter's worth of credits for my summer classes. I got Cs in four economics courses. Cs are better than I had been doing, but they were unlike the As I had gotten in high school.

CHAPTER 19

LEARNING THAT ANTIDEPRESSANTS CAN BE FOR THE LONG-TERM

During the fall of 1982, I lived in a dorm on the UW campus. I managed to pass two classes because I usually stayed on my antidepressant Asendin.

Asendin seemed like such a miracle that I thought I should have gotten it sooner. I asked Dr. Haglund if she would testify in a medical malpractice trial against Dr. Kelly and Dr. Holley for not giving me Asendin sooner.

She said, "No."

I said, "Why not?"

She gave a weak excuse for the other doctors, saying, "Manic depression is hard to diagnose."

No, it's not. The list of symptoms is in the back of this book and had been known for years. They were identified by Dr. Emil Kraepelin, who lived from 1856 to 1926.

I guess doctors won't testify against each other because they fear some form of retaliation. They fear being shunned by the medical community. That is my guess.

I figured that if I couldn't get my current doctor to testify against my old doctors, I didn't have much of a case. I'd have to go hunting for another doctor to be an expert witness. I was afraid I'd get the same negative response.

I was on 300 mg of antidepressant Asendin, 1200 mg of mood leveler lithium, and the side effect drug Cogentin. After a while, I quit taking the lithium and Cogentin because of the drowsiness side effect. I continued to take the Asendin.

When I saw Dr. Haglund, she asked, "How are you?"

I usually said, "I'm drowsy, and I have the low- interest-in-romance side effect."

She usually asked, "Are you dating?"

"No. How am I going to tell women that I have a mental illness?"

"You don't have to tell them right away."

"But what do I say when I do tell them, and what do I say when they ask why it's taken me so long to graduate?"

She'd say something useless like, "Just say you were sick."

I said, "Besides, I have erectile dysfunction."

At first, Dr. Haglund didn't believe me when I told her about this low-interest-in-romance side effect. This was because antidepressant Asendin was new on the market, and I was probably her first and only patient for whom she had ever prescribed it. If this side effect had been known, it probably would not have gotten FDA approval. Most antidepressants available at that time give just a trace of delayed orgasm, which does not harm your love life as badly as Asendin. Also, I was just about the only patient she was seeing then because she was mostly a lecturer and administrator. She was semiretired, so she wasn't a good doctor for seeing patients, because to be good at something, you have to do it all the time. She saw very few patients, so her skills were not sharp.

She always said, "You should start dating."

While having a significant other is usually helpful and a great morale booster in a number of ways, it is not a cure. A significant other can, however, provide daily feedback on how your meds are working. Are you cheerful, uncheerful, or somewhere in-between? Are you crabby or friendly?

The dorm I was living in during fall of 1982 was an all men's dorm, but we ate our meals with a coed dorm. I usually sat with the guys on my floor. One day, I got up enough nerve to sit with one of the prettiest women at the dorm. There was an empty space next to her, and I just sat down and said, "Hi."

Her name was Bridget. I developed a big crush on her almost immediately. She was smart, vivacious, and pretty. She already had a steady boyfriend, though, so we were just friends.

Of course, I still wanted a steady girlfriend of my own. I made arrangements to move to a coed dorm on the other side of campus for winter quarter 1983. Dr. Haglund approved of this. I knew Asendin was making a big difference because I tried going without it a couple of times during the fall quarter of 1982. I failed some tests those days without Asendin and ended up with two Cs and two Ds for grades. I did well when I stayed on the Asendin.

During Christmas vacation, my father Lee, stepmother Connie, and brothers Rick, Johnny, Steve, and I went skiing for four days. Skiing was okay the first day, but then I ran out of Asendin, and I started to feel like doing nothing. Without Asendin, depression returned immediately. I skied maybe one hour the last two days. We were in a small town, so I couldn't immediately get a refill.

We got back in town a few days before school started. When I finally got to see Dr. Haglund, classes had already started, and I hadn't been to class yet. I was sitting in my new dorm room doing nothing. I was that depressed without Asendin. I was feeling so badly unmotivated that I was not going to class. I was preoccupied with past troubles. I was having trouble getting out of my bed in the morning because I didn't have Asendin to treat my depression.

When I saw Dr. Haglund, she asked, "How do you feel?

I said, "Not too bad."

Haglund asked, "Do you want to die?"

I said, "No, I want to live."

"You don't need any more antidepressant."

"Yes, I do. I need some more antidepressant Asendin. I haven't been going to class. I'm not motivated!"

"Try going without it. I'll give you some next time if you need it."

"Please," I begged.

"No," was her only reply.

I saw her about two weeks later. Meanwhile, my depression got worse. I went to a few classes, but I couldn't concentrate. When I went down to meals in my dorm, I often sat with some women and introduced myself, but I said that I was manic depressive, and that turned them off. The more politically correct term is now "bipolar affective disorder." It sounds better than "manic depression."

When I started to take antidepressant Asendin again, I immediately felt better. I quit thinking about past troubles so much. I started going to class. There were about four weeks left in the winter quarter, and I managed to get a C in one of my three classes. I dropped and flunked the other two.

I still was occasionally having lunch with Bridget. Her mother had had a stroke in February of the same type that my mother had. We talked about that for a long time and became good friends. She was the first good friend I had made in years. It was fun.

After I was feeling better at the end of winter quarter, my roommate,

Walter, convinced me to go to Mazatlan, Mexico for a spring break vacation. Because I was feeling better—in spite of the fact that I didn't have anyone to go with—I signed up to go by myself. I wouldn't really be by myself, because they would assign me roommates, and the town would be loaded with other American college kids, partying up a storm. I went and met some people on the plane, roomed with them, hit the beach and the clubs for a week, and had a good time. I didn't drink, because I figured I shouldn't because of my antidepressant Asendin. I met some people from all over the United States, and I enjoyed myself. Asendin helped a lot.

Also in Mazatlan, I ran into Doug Bossard. He was a guy from the University of Puget Sound who I knew from the swim team there.

I went back up to Seattle and started spring quarter. My classes were on abnormal psychology, statistics, and expository writing. I was on the full 300 mg of antidepressant Asendin and no mood leveler lithium. I sat with the guys on my dorm floor for meals.

I was a lot better off with Asendin than without it. My intellect worked. I did have another friend named Rachel, a woman I knew from UPS. She was living in Seattle then. We went to a lot of movies. We were just friends, and that was fine with me. A person needs friends.

I was still seeing my friend, Jane Eggers, once a month for pizza. She was the one who had been my resident advisor sophomore year at UPS. I had called her when I was really depressed in the winter of 1982. I saw her once a month, and it helped give me someone to talk to. She was also the head of the Seattle Mental Health Association. She told me about the Washington Manic Depressive Association. They had support groups.

When I went to some of the support groups, in a way I was glad to hear other people's stories about what they did when they were manic, but I sure didn't want to be like them. I was usually one of the youngest in the group, and I didn't want to end up like the other group members when I was their age. These people were divorced, unemployed, broke, and on welfare. I didn't like going to the meetings, because these were not the type of people I liked to hang around with. I did go several times, though, and I got some literature about manic depression, read it all, and learned a little about the medications.

The end of spring quarter came, and I had stayed "undepressed" enough to get two Bs and a C, thanks to 300 mg of antidepressant Asendin. Let's hear it for the medication!

CHAPTER 20

LOUSY MEDICAL PRACTICE LEADS TO MY CONTEMPLATING SUICIDE

In the summer of 1983, I asked my psychiatrist, Dr. Haglund, if I could reduce my antidepressant Asendin dose to 200 mg per day. This would cause less of the side effect of low interest in romance and less drowsiness. There would also be less of the side effects of dry mouth, dry nose, and dry eyes. The main thing I was concerned about was getting rid of the low interest in romance. Dr. Haglund said I could reduce the dose. This would later prove to be a big mistake. On a lower dose, the side effects were reduced, and I didn't get extremely depressed right away.

Since March 1983, I had been seeing a psychologist named Donald Mulcrone in addition to seeing Dr. Haglund who was a psychiatrist. Psychologists are not medical doctors and therefore cannot prescribe drugs. They believe in talk therapy called psychotherapy. In 1983, many of them were anti-medication. That was stupid.

I went to Mulcrone with the idea that he could help me forget about past troubles and that he could help me to know how to start a relationship with a woman, in spite of the fact that I would have to tell her that I was manic depressive. Also, in March—when I first started seeing Mr. Mulcrone—he said that it would be good to treat my depression with psychotherapy, instead of medicine. That way I would not have the side effects of antidepressant Asendin.

Mr. Mulcrone seemed to have no system of therapy except to tell me to ask out any woman I mentioned. He was of little use.

As the summer wore on, I began to get depressed and started having some trouble in my classes. I became obsessed with the depressive fear of getting manic. I was depressed about the possibility of getting manic in the future! Dr. Haglund, the psychiatrist, and I thought the fear was legitimate. Mr. Mulcrone, the psychologist, thought the fear was not legitimate. He thought he should get rid of my obsessive fear of mania by arguing with me.

Mulcrone said, "You're not going to get manic."

I said, "I could."

"You will not."

"I could."

"You will not."

"I could. I have before."

"I doubt it. I've never seen you manic."

"You've only seen me for four months. I was manic two years ago in 1981."

"I never saw you that way."

"I was manic."

"I don't know that."

"I was manic. Don't you believe me?"

Mulcrone said, "I've never seen you manic."

"I was in the hospital for being manic three times."

"I've never seen you manic."

I thought Mulcrone was annoying.

A few days later, I saw Dr. Haglund, the medical doctor and

psychiatrist, who thought the fear of mania was legitimate, so we started to discuss putting me on the mood leveler Tegretol, which is supposed to prevent mania. It is an alternative med to the mood leveler lithium. Both are supposed to help prevent mania. I didn't like lithium, because of the drowsiness and muscle tremors it gave me. Nobody realized that my fear of mania was just a symptom of depression.

So, I started to take Tegretol to prevent mania in addition to my antidepressant Asendin for depression. I had feared Tegretol because it had a bunch of awful things listed as possible side effects. I felt I had to have it to prevent mania. I didn't want to get manic at a job and get fired. I didn't want to get manic in a marriage and get dumped. I was really obsessed with these fears.

Dr. Haglund had said, "Just try Tegretol to prevent mania for a while, and if it's too awful, you can go off it."

When I first started mood leveler Tegretol, it put my speech on a one-second time delay. It was some weird neurological phenomenon that made my words come out one second after I told them to come out, caused by the combination of antidepressant Asendin and Tegretol. I had to not listen to myself or I would get confused. It was like calling a radio station and being on a seven-second time delay, only this was just one second. The disc jockey always has to tell callers, "Turn down your radio!"

I had to give a short speech in front of a class with my voice echoing a second later. I was really nervous. Afterward, I asked the teacher if I sounded clear enough. She said I sounded clear but nervous. I was nervous because I had never spoken in front of a group with my voice on echo.

Later, mood leveler Tegretol made me uncoordinated, so Dr. Haglund told me to get off it. I still had the depressive, obsessive fear of getting manic. This obsession was a symptom of depression due to not enough antidepressant Asendin, but neither Dr. Haglund nor Mr. Mulcrone nor I knew it. I didn't realize this until later, when I went back on the full dose of Asendin. Once Tegretol was disqualified, I reluctantly went back on mood leveler lithium, which helps prevent mania.

Mr. Mulcrone continued telling me that my fear of mania was unfounded. "I've never seen you manic," he said.

He also said, "One survey in a rural area showed that there was no mental illness there in a six month period." He said, "Lithium has never been proven to work. It's just a theory someone has, so there is no use taking it to prevent mania." Last but not least, he said, "Some experts believe there is no such thing as mental illness. People just have different ways of looking at things, so you don't need lithium." Of course, I knew it then, and I know it now: he was a terrible psychologist. I went to him a few more times, though, hoping *he* would straighten out.

So, I was on mood leveler lithium and 200 mg of antidepressant Asendin, and I was pessimistic about my future. It was August and I had gotten Cs for the first summer session of school. Now I needed only two classes in order to graduate. Mr. Mulcrone had encouraged me to call the Seattle Area Jewish Dating Service to get some dates. I did that, and I got a date with a woman for lunch on campus. I was feeling really awful and pessimistic about everything and everyone at this time. The exceptions were my friends Bridget, Rachel, and Jane. I was friends with these three women, but not lovers.

I had this blind date for lunch with the woman I had met through the dating service, but I hardly said anything because I was so depressed. She talked, and I pretended to listen and care. Then I went to my dorm and contemplated suicide.

I thought about the low-interest-in-romance side effect from Asendin and the way I felt, and the fact that I could get manic, and I felt like the future was hopeless. This blind date was a stress. I kept comparing how the theoretical healthy me would have handled it. I would have been so charming and lovable. Actually, I thought, the healthy me would've been married by now. I felt the healthy me would never return. I thought of better meds, but I was sure that would never happen. I thought the healthy sixteen-year-old me would have been able to attract a girlfriend, but I thought that the healthy me would never return. I feared I would never be able to hold a job for long because I would get manic too often. Therefore, there was no use living. I thought about killing myself with a gun because that would be the surest way. I was thinking about the location of some gun stores, and I decided I should kill myself in the parking ramp where I parked my car. Then I thought, I didn't want to be a mess for someone to clean up, so I better not do it. Then I thought about the fact that my friends and family would rather have me alive, so I shouldn't do it. Also, maybe they would have better medications someday. I was doing this contemplating in the lounge of my dorm. I decided not to do it, thinking maybe there would be better drugs one day. Then I went back to my room and cried. I was crying at the thought that I almost died.

Knowing that I was on 200 mg of antidepressant Asendin and that 300 mg worked better, I took 600 mg of Asendin that afternoon because according to the package insert that gives prescribing information for Asendin, 600 mg is the most you can safely take of Asendin in one day. For anything above 400 mg, you are supposed to be in the hospital, but I thought I better take 600 mg to save my life.

After I took the 600 mg of antidepressant Asendin, I called Glenn Simco. He was the head and founder of the Washington Depressive & Manic Depressive Association. I told him I had been suicidal, and he said I should call my doctor.

He said, "Remember, you want to kill the disease. You don't want to kill you."

Then, I called Dr. Haglund at home, and after reassuring her that I was not going to do it, she said, "Come to my office at nine tomorrow morning."

My reading of package inserts, *The Physician's Desk Reference,* and other books about medication is what has helped me to be fairly healthy today. Reading about medication helps and so does having good friends who can give feedback on how your meds seem to be working each day.

The next day I went to Dr. Haglund's office, and after talking for a while she said, "I'm going to switch your antidepressant around."

I said, "No, no, just give me some more Asendin. I was on 200 mg, and that's what caused the problem. I was fine on 300 mg. Just give me some more Asendin."

Dr. Haglund said, "Oh no, let's switch. That Asendin is a bad drug."

After a few more minutes of arguing like this, I said, "No, give me Asendin, or I'll go to another doctor."

She said, "Okay."

Of course, given that my life was at stake, and given that antidepressant Asendin works at 300 mg, giving me something else at that point would have been extremely lousy medical practice.

I got my prescription for antidepressant Asendin filled, took 500 mg for a few days, and felt much better after only three days. During these three days, I felt bad that I had nobody reasonable to talk to. I knew that I had many old friends and a few new friends who cared about me, but I didn't tell any of them that I was suicidal. I knew they would help me if they could, but I thought they could not help. I didn't want to ruin their day by making them worry about me. I didn't want to be a bigger chore than I already was.

I remember going to my classes and thinking the people there didn't realize that I had almost died. I figured someday I would have people who care and I would be healthy, so I could tell the story, but it would be past tense, so it wouldn't upset them. I knew the antidepressant Asendin would work. Those three days I had lots of side effects, including dry mouth, dry nose, dry eyes, and drowsiness, but I knew Asendin would work. After three days, I lowered the dose back to the usual 300 mg and felt okay. Thank goodness for the medicine! After a week, suicide was far from my mind. This clearly shows that manic depression is a biochemical illness. The medication restored my brain chemicals to a more normal level.

Later I went to see the psychologist, Mr. Mulcrone, and I told him about the afternoon I had contemplated suicide. In the evening of the same day that I contemplated suicide, I had gone to a movie with Rachel Moeller.

Mr. Mulcrone asked, "Did you feel better when you were with Rachel?"

I said, "Yeah."

He said, "Well that should tell you something."

I said angrily, "Like what? I'm supposed to have people around me all the time or I'll commit suicide? It was the drugs not working at too low a dose."

Mr. Mulcrone said, "Well this incident should show you the value of personal relationships."

He was saying, it seemed, "I told you so, I told you so. I told you, you need to make friends. Suicidal thoughts are a normal reaction to being stuck by yourself for twenty-four hours. This is what you get and deserve when you don't make more friends."

What an idiot he was.

Of course, his statement was extremely lousy medical practice, and I knew it then. I quit seeing Mr. Mulcrone shortly thereafter.

Later, over a soda with a psychiatric nursing graduate student who lived on my dorm floor, I said, "Happiness can be found in a bottle of Asendin."

He said, "No, no, you have to create a life for yourself that is rewarding."

This conversation went on for a while, but I wouldn't budge from my point of view that happiness can be found in a bottle of antidepressant Asendin.

I finished my classes and passed, so I graduated with a B.A. in economics. I didn't bother attending the graduation exercises.

I quit worrying about mania once I was back on 300 mg of Asendin instead of 200 mg.

CHAPTER 21

BRAINS YES, PERSONALITY NO

I got a part-time job as a pizza delivery driver for Dave's Pizza near the UW campus. It was a mildly amusing job but not very profitable because it put a lot of miles on my car. The mileage reimbursement they gave for using your own car was not enough. I kept the job for two years, so I could put it on my resume after I graduated from Seattle Area Technical Vocational Institute, which I started in December 1983.

I started the year-and-a-half course at Seattle Area Technical Vocational Institute to learn computer repair. I had sent out a bunch of resumes after I graduated from UW, but after getting lots of rejection letters, I had given up at finding a job using my economics degree. I had heard a lot of stories of some high school classmates of mine getting jobs repairing computers. So, I signed up for the computer technician program at the Vo-Tech. I had always looked down on Vo-Tech as the place people go if they aren't bright enough to get into college. Now I saw it as a practical option. My biggest fear was that I would be too drowsy to stay awake in class. I was on antidepressant Asendin and mood leveler lithium. Luckily I stayed awake in class in December and made it to January when I was not on mood leveler lithium and was therefore less drowsy. I dropped the lithium because lithium plus antidepressant Asendin caused too much drowsiness. I kept taking the Asendin, and it made my concentration good enough to get nearly straight A grades.

Antidepressants, by the way, are not addictive. They are safe, legal, prescribed, non-addictive, mind-altering drugs. They cheer you up. Also, they are not anesthesia. They do not numb you. They make you more alert and more conscious. They cheer you up. In addition, antidepressants have no street value.

Some psychiatric medications are addictive. The anti-anxiety drugs Valium and Xanax are addictive. They are different from antidepressants.

In the beginning of the Vo-Tech program in computer repair, I had told two fellow students about my manic depression and the fact that I was on medication. This is because they noticed my drowsiness. One of them quit the program, so the only person in my class who knew was the other. I don't think he told anyone, but for the rest of the program, I was sure that I was nice to him because I was afraid otherwise he would tell people.

From 1984 to 1985, during vacations from computer repair school, I tried different antidepressants, hoping for no depression while decreasing the low-interest-in-romance side effect. They didn't work. It was very lousy medical practice to try them for less than six weeks. Some antidepressants suddenly work the sixth week of the full dose. I didn't know that at the time. None of the alternative drugs worked during the vacations, so I went back to antidepressant Asendin so I could get As (or at least Cs) in school. Also, on Asendin I felt better. Trying a new antidepressant for only two weeks was two weeks of misery for nothing. It was two weeks of being fairly close to crying all day. Thankfully, Asendin worked the first day. Asendin was different from the other antidepressants I tried because it worked the first day. So, the Sunday night at the end of a vacation, I went back to Asendin. I woke up Monday feeling okay.

It would immediately cheer me up. School usually started again the next day. I then regarded the new drug as being no good, even though it had not been given a fair six-week trial.

At one point, I boosted my dose of antidepressant Asendin to 350 mg up from 300 mg to get rid of some negative feelings. I felt better right away. I was less irritable. At 350 mg, the side effects were all worse, but they bothered me less because I was in so much of a better mood. I decided to stick with 350 mg because I was mentally so much better. There was one problem: I got hungrier. I gained about twenty pounds in two weeks, and ten more in the next month.

I tried to be nicer to all my classmates now that I was in a better mood.

A girlfriend would have been nice, although by this time I was aware that having a romance was not the way to treat or the way to prevent manic depression. In the winter of 1985, I had three dates with a woman I met who was a waitress at a restaurant I went to. Her name was Shelly. We went out to dinner, had a good conversation, and then I drove her back to her apartment and we kissed in my car. I remember telling myself to try to act like I would be acting if only I felt normal, but of course I didn't feel normal. I still had the awful low-interest-in-romance side effect. I thought, *Act like you're enjoying it,* but I wasn't. It just seemed stupid. This kissing was way less exciting than the kissing I had done when I was normal. It was also less exciting than the kissing I had done while depressed and untreated. At least with antidepressant Asendin, I could get As in school instead of Fs. My intellect worked.

After two minutes of this unexciting kissing, I said, "Good night" or something and we called it an evening.

I would guess now that she would've preferred more enthusiasm and for me to ask if I could come up to her apartment. On our next date, I forget what we did, but then I kissed her again unenthusiastically. On our third date, she walked out on me in the middle of a racquetball game when I tried to tell her she had to get out of the way to let the other person's shot hit the front wall. That was the end of that.

During this period of my life, I went to support groups of the Washington Depressive and Manic Depressive Association once in awhile, but I usually considered myself too well to go there. At group meetings, I got a reputation as someone who tries a lot of different antidepressants. They called me Mr. Antidepressant.

Things at my house were calm. My dad and his wife, Connie, were easy to get along with.

In June 1985, I graduated from the Vo-Tech computer repair program in a four-way tie for the highest grades in the class. The class had twenty-four people.

Asendin stopped depression, but not totally. I saw room for improvement. I still second-guessed myself all day. Things like: What channel on television would I be watching if I were healthy? Which brand of soap would I be using if I were healthy? What would I be eating right now if I were healthy? What would I be saying right now if I were healthy? Having so many questions was a symptom. Never mind the answers to the questions.

Now that I am healthier, I don't second-guess myself all day.

I still was friends with Rachel, who I knew from the University of Puget Sound. We went to movies or on walks. We were just friends, but we saw each other about every other week. Among our many conversations was one that went like this:

I said, "Oh man, I'm so drowsy. I just hate these drugs. I don't know what drug to try next."

She said, "I am so disgusted. I am so fat. I've gained five pounds in the past week. This is ridiculous!"

She was not fat.

After thinking about it for a few seconds, I said, "Okay, Rachel.

I won't talk about my drugs, and you don't say you're fat."

CHAPTER 22

I WANT A NEW DRUG

Using my Vo-Tech diploma, I got hired July 5, 1985, for a job repairing copiers. I was slow to learn. My drowsiness, poor concentration, and irritable mood were a problem, so I was fired in January 1986. I had gotten good grades at the Vo-Tech because I did three hours of homework each night. At the copy machine repair job, there wasn't really a way to do some work at home, so my academic success did not translate into success at work.

At the support groups, I was continuing my reputation for being Mr. Antidepressant. People at the meetings went on and on about how unhappy they were, and often others would say nothing, so I would say, "Try an antidepressant."

Sometimes, people said they were thinking of suicide, and everyone else in the group would just sit there.

I would say, "Get your doctor to prescribe an antidepressant."

I may have saved some lives.

I learned later that antidepressants can sometimes lift your mood up too high and cause you to get manic. Still, they have to be tried if you are depressed, and especially if you are suicidal. I got on some people's nerves for giving too much advice. I didn't emphasize that you had to check with your doctor before switching medication. I thought people knew that. I liked going to the support groups to help other people.

If I saw people doing better than I was doing, I asked them what medication they were on. In that way, the support group helped me.

CHAPTER 23

HANGING AROUND

I applied for unemployment compensation, and in March 1986, I got it.

For recreation, my cousin Laura Felber had convinced me to go to international folk dancing. Laura had decided I needed to be more social, so I should try dancing. I started going in October 1985. There were some attractive women there, so I decided to keep going. I had trouble learning the dances, but I tried.

The dancing was set up so that there was teaching from 7:00 to 8:00 p.m. and requests from 8:00 to 10:00 p.m, every Tuesday night. There are about two hundred different dances.

Two women I liked seeing at international folk dancing were Jenny and Debbie. They were students at the University of Washington. They talked to me a lot, unlike most of the people there, and when I told them I was manic depressive, they didn't seem to mind. Sometimes we'd go out to eat after dancing. I really liked Jenny, but she wanted to only be friends. That was all right. Friends are important.

During the week, I started volunteering at the office of the Washington Depressive and Manic Depressive Association (WDMDA). The office was all volunteer except that Glenn Simco, who was in charge, got about two hundred dollars a month. All the money for the organization was donated, and nobody donated very much. My big project was typing the names of everyone who had ever been at a support group meeting into the computer, so that we could have a mailing list. Also, there were many other assorted manic depressives who hung around in the office that I got to know.

I was in better shape than most of the other manic depressives who worked at the office because I was on an antidepressant that worked. However, I wouldn't usually stay in the office very long because I couldn't stand it. This is because I was still unhappy. I didn't want to make a big commitment to WDMDA, because I didn't want manic depression to be my full-time job. I didn't want working on it to be my sole purpose in life or my sole source of social contacts.

Meanwhile, Dr. Haglund was bugging me to try an MAOI antidepressant. I was balking because a person was supposed to be on no drug at all for a while in-between a tricyclic antidepressant like Asendin and an MAOI antidepressant. On no drug at all, I could kill myself. Dr. Haglund said it was not that risky to take one a few days after the other, but I refused to risk my life for another antidepressant that probably wouldn't work. Once, I was going to try to make the switch from Asendin to MAOI antidepressant Nardil, but after a few days off Asendin, my fear that I would be suicidal made me go back on Asendin before I ever took any Nardil.

Then Dr. Haglund made a classic stupid statement, "If you weren't so pessimistic, it would be easier to treat your depression."

I was still living at home with Dad and my stepmother Connie. They didn't bug me. It wasn't that bad. I tried to stay distant, and that worked okay. I usually ate dinner with them. However, I ate quickly and did not talk to them or listen to them. They spoke to each other. I was glad they didn't demand attention from me. My dad's behavior was really just fine at this time, but I felt I should stay distant so he wouldn't get too attached to me.

I had taken the written test to be a mail carrier about two years earlier, and the post office had finally gotten to my name on the waiting list. I started work as a mail carrier in May 1986. The job has two parts, sorting and delivering. I was on 350 mg of antidepressant Asendin. Even though Asendin helps a lot, my concentration was still not very good. I still thought a lot about the arguments I used to have with my dad, instead of paying attention to my work. Thinking about the arguments was just a symptom. My dad had been a nice guy since 1982. I got fired from the post office after a couple months for being too slow.

In September and October of 1986 I continued to volunteer for WDMDA and answered phone calls from people who said things like, "Hi, I just ah, took the CPI (California Personality Inventory) for the fifth time." (The CPI is a very long personality test. It takes a long time to fill out, and is not necessary once a person has been diagnosed as depressive. A much shorter test is appropriate once a diagnosis has been made.)

I asked, "Why did you just take it again?"

The caller said, "Well, I just moved in from out of town, so I went to a new psychiatrist."

"What did your new doctor say?"

"My doctor said I was depressed."

"Did he give you any antidepressants?"

"No."

"Have you been given antidepressants by previous doctors?"

"Yes, but they didn't work."

"Well, I can give you the name of a group of doctors who will give you antidepressants. One of them might work." (I still failed to emphasize trying all the antidepressants for at least six weeks. This is because I still didn't know better, thanks to Dr. Haglund failing to tell me.)

"Well, all I do is go from doctor to doctor and get these drugs, and they never help."

"Well, there are about ten antidepressants, and if one doesn't work, you've got to try another. Just try these doctors. They will make an effort. You probably haven't been on a large enough dose. Also, come to our support groups. I'll send you some literature."

"All right, I suppose. Bye."

We got about one phone call per half hour, and we usually told them about our support groups and mailed them literature. I still felt stuck in a crummy phase of my life. Working at the office was fairly boring.

For recreation, I was now hanging around with a guy named Howard Schultz. He was a healthy individual I had met at a Jewish singles party.

We were hanging around at the party, and I said to Howard, "I am out of work because I was fired for being too slow because I am manic depressive."

He said, "I have trouble holding jobs too because my bosses are jerks. I think my bosses are manic depressives," he said jokingly.

The day after the party, Howard called me and asked, "What are you doing?"

I said, "I'm just sitting at home watching the news. What are you doing?

"Oh, I just got off of work. I'm just doing this job until I find something better."

We talked for a while, he about his jobs, me about manic depression.

We started doing a few things together like eating at restaurants. Howard also was a collector of 78 rpm records, and lots of other old stuff. He went to estate sales to buy these old things. On a couple weekends, I went with him to estate sales and looked at the stuff for sale while he looked at the old records. He liked the music on old records from the 1930s and 1940s.

CHAPTER 24

I REALLY NEED A NEW DRUG

In September and October of 1986, I sent out falsified resumes in an attempt to get another job in the electronic technician field. I had to lie so that they wouldn't know I was fired from my last two jobs. I had no luck really, so in November I took a near minimum wage job at a photocopy shop. I was already twenty-seven, so my coworkers and boss were a few years younger than I, but I didn't mind. I was working 6 p.m. to midnight on weekdays. That was thirty hours per week. I would mostly ring stuff up at the cash register and clean the place at closing time.

Then an electronics firm that I had applied to called. They wanted to interview me for a job repairing circuit boards.

With the lies from my resume memorized, I went to the interview, and luckily, the interviewer didn't really ask me any questions about my past. He just told me about the company and asked me when I could start. He said I would be permanent part-time, and then I could work my way up to full-time. My hours were 1:00 p.m. to 5:00 p.m. So, I could still work at the photocopy shop.

For a few weeks, I was working both jobs, a total of fifty hours a week. That's the most I ever worked. I started to displease my boss at the electronics job because I was not repairing enough boards per day.

There was homework I could have done to learn the circuit much more quickly, but I never found time to get that homework done. When I started to get in trouble at the electronics job, I quit the photocopy job in order to have time to study the circuits, but it was too late. In mid-January, I was fired from the electronics job for being too slow. Much of the problem was not the lack of doing my homework; it was mostly a case of poor concentration. Three hundred and fifty milligrams of antidepressant Asendin only works so well.

In March, I raised my dose of antidepressant Asendin from 350 mg to 400 mg. I immediately felt better than I had ever felt on 350 mg. The dreaded low-interest-in-romance side effect was a little worse, but I didn't mind it as much, because I was in such a better mood. I also didn't mind any of life's problems as much. People noticed that I was in a better mood. Things seemed easier and more fun. Dr. Haglund was upset that I changed my dose on my own, but she agreed I was in a better mood, so she let me continue.

Besides visiting my few friends, most of my time was spent just hanging around watching television. I watched the news several times a day. I watched talk shows. Often I would try a new antidepressant for two weeks, as I have described before.

I did have a few friends. Howard Schultz called me every day. We'd go out to eat sometimes or rent a video. He was still struggling to find a job he could hold.

My father suggested that I quit trying new antidepressants and get a job.

I said to him what I always said at support groups: "I am in search of the magical antidepressant without side effects."

Dad said, "It's not good to sit around without a job."

I thought that I would never improve to the degree that I have. Depression makes one pessimistic about everything. I was pessimistic about my recovery from depression. I did think I could improve to a degree. That's why I kept trying different medications.

My doctor never said anything that indicated that she thought I was going to get as much better as I have. She *did* think I could improve to some extent. That's why she kept prescribing different medications for me.

Taking my dad's suggestion, in August 1987, I applied (false application info, of course) to the Dave's Pizza on Mercer Island. I had worked there before, but the turnover was so high that nobody there was recognizable. I applied to be a phone order taker. It was a job I already knew, and at four dollars per hour, it paid better than delivering. When you deliver, you destroy your car by putting a lot of miles on it, and that subtracts greatly from your pay. I told them I just wanted to answer phones, and I'd consider making pizzas (although I didn't think I could make pizzas fast enough), but I did not want to deliver. They hired me, and I started working there answering phones. I worked about four or five nights a week during the dinner rush, answering phones. It was dreary, but I did the job well enough.

Dreary thought patterns were preoccupying my mind and slowing down my work, in spite of antidepressant Asendin's help. These were the same sorts of strings of depressive thoughts that I mentioned before. I would hope for "magic wishes" or miracles by God coming to earth and totally curing me.

In September, the Mercer Island High School class of 1977 held a ten-year reunion. It was reassuring to know that all these people still existed out there and that most were having fun and progressing through life normally. People still looked pretty much the same. I talked to a lot of people, and they were friendly. It was good being with a group of people who remembered primarily the healthy me. A few expected me to be a doctor or a lawyer, but I had to tell them the truth. People listened and many told me that their boyfriend, father, or brother-in-law was manic depressive. Melanie Carson wasn't there. That was good because I had planned to avoid her.

A few days later, Dr. Haglund again wanted me to try the antidepressant Nardil. But before I went through weeks of depression, probably for nothing, I wanted to talk to some other people on Nardil who were doing well on it.

Dr. Haglund said, "I have hundreds and hundreds of patients on Nardil."

I said, "Name three."

She could only name one, so I asked her to get permission from that patient for me to call her. A few days later, Dr. Haglund gave me that patient's phone number.

I called her.

She went on and on about how depressed she "had been" but said she was now happy. I was hoping to hear more about how good life was now, but instead I got gory details of how horrible life had been.

I decided her life now was not so happy because she was preoccupied with the past.

I told Dr. Haglund that when she could find me three manic depressives who were doing well while on antidepressant Nardil, who had jobs and significant others, then I'd try it.

I was working about twenty hours per week at Dave's Pizza, answering the phones. My concentration wasn't very good. I couldn't take an order while walking over to put up the previous order. The phones had long extension cords. However, I couldn't remember the second order long enough to write it down ten seconds later, rather than right away. While walking over to put up the first order, I would forget the second order.

Most of my coworkers were younger than I, but I didn't mind. I was a little bit depressed all the time, so I wasn't too popular. I wasn't cheerful enough. There were a couple guys who were friendly to me. In February 1988, I mentioned to them that I was manic depressive. That was the first I had spoken of it. I didn't give them the gory details, but one of them said his girlfriend was on the antidepressant Elavil. That was nice to know. It was nice to know that a depressive had a boyfriend.

For recreation, I still went to international folk dancing, but my concentration was so bad that I could still only do the easiest dances.

I continued to attend WDMDA meetings and sometimes helped type the newsletter into the computer. Support group meeting space was donated by a hospital. They let us meet in a conference room or cafeteria for free.

The meetings were free, and conducted on a self-help and peer-led basis. At a support group meeting, first we read the group guidelines, and then we went around the circle of about eight, one by one, to introduce ourselves. Then it was open for free-flowing discussion. We wore nametags with first name only. I will describe a typical meeting.

A middle-aged guy dressed neatly in blue jeans and not smiling said, "Hi, I'm Joe. I'll be the facilitator tonight. I've been diagnosed with this illness for about ten years. I've had some manic episodes, and now I'm in sort of a depression. My work is getting more difficult, and I think the stress from work is making things worse. My ex-wife is giving me a hard time also. With that, I'll pass." (Looks left, looks right.) "Jill, do you want to go next?"

Jill opened her mouth and took a breath but didn't say anything.

Todd said slowly and hesitantly, "I'll go. I'm Todd, I've had this illness for a while. I, um, think it's serious because it has slowed down my memory and, um, energy." Sadly, he continued, "I don't know if that is from the illness or side effects of the medication. Otherwise I'm ah, um, doing okay. I'll pass."

Next to Todd sat Stephanie. Stephanie was grossly overweight, and was wearing big stretch pants.

Sounding upset, Stephanie said, "Ooh, I didn't know if I was going to make it here tonight. I've been having such a rough time. I was so depressed. I've been crying all day (sob), and my doctor hasn't even called me back yet. Also, my meds have made me gain seventy pounds." Stephanie was silent for a moment and stared at the floor.

Joe the facilitator said, "What happened?"

"I just got kicked out of my apartment. Now I have to go live with my mother."

Joe said, "Okay, we will come back to you after introductions and talk about it more."

I said, "Hi. I'm Bill and I've been manic depressive since November of 1976. I'm stuck in the depressed phase, so I'm looking for the magical antidepressant without side effects. I'm on Asendin now, and it helps, but it doesn't help enough. It also has a lot of side effects. Right now, I'm just working at Dave's Pizza, answering the phones. That's all for now."

We then moved to the next person. It was Kelly. She was in her early thirties, was dressed neatly in blue jeans, and she didn't smile. Kelly said, "I don't really know what to do. I'm worried about my fifteen-year-old daughter, Andrea. I think my illness is affecting her. See, she doesn't have a father, just like me. She might be taking after me. I never knew my real father. Then my stepfather abused me until I was about twelve, when my mother kicked him out. Then a year later, my mother committed suicide. I went to live with my aunt and uncle. They were very religious, and I couldn't stand it. I ran away with my boyfriend when I was sixteen and pregnant with Andrea. Things were okay for a few years, but we really had a codependent relationship. We were really dysfunctional parents for Andrea when she was little. We both drank. We never got legally married. My boyfriend got killed in a one-car accident when Andrea was just ten. I know he was drunk. I started to get depressed somewhere around that time. Then I freaked out and was in the hospital for being manic, except I might be schizophrenic. Now Andrea likes *boys* and stays out late. She goes to *parties.* She doesn't listen to me. I'm afraid she is depressed. It's dangerous for kids these days."

We finished going around the circle, and then we opened things up for discussion, going first to Stephanie to try to help her.

I often said, "You need an antidepressant."

A few people argued with me and said that drugs are not the solution. People said that there are things in Stephanie's environment that need changing because that is what is making her unhappy.

I said, "If we weren't so biologically depressed, we wouldn't mind our environment so much."

Usually everyone there was in one degree of depression or another. Basically, they all needed to boost the dose of their antidepressant or find another, I thought. At that time, I didn't pay much attention to the fact that antidepressants can often make a manic depressive go up too high—beyond normal—into the manic phase. Still, antidepressants need to be tried.

People at the support groups usually just spoke up in no particular order after the introduction. Sometimes one person would state a problem and several would comment on that. Then another other would state a problem and several would comment on that. A good facilitator would not talk much more than anyone else. He would maybe call on someone who was being quiet to make sure the quiet person got a chance to speak.

Our support group meetings lasted about an hour and a half, once a week. I went to learn from other people, to teach other people, and to be sociable. It was better than television.

In March 1988, my antidepressant Asendin quit working. It had worked for six years, and now it gradually quit working. Four hundred milligrams had been my usual dose. I started to feel worse. I worried more and thought about crying more. I boosted the dose to 450 mg and then 500. It didn't help. I went to see Dr. Haglund.

I said, "We have a major problem. Asendin has quit working." This was a major problem because I had tried most of the other sixteen antidepressants and they hadn't worked. I was afraid I would be suicidal in two weeks. We agreed I would try antidepressant Norpramine again, and I said, "I should try it for six weeks."

Dr. Haglund agreed.

I had heard at support groups that they can suddenly start working the sixth week.

As I have said, over the previous five years I had tried about twelve of the antidepressants for two weeks. This was in an effort to find one with a less severe low-interest-in-romance side effect. I would lie around obsessing about the past and listening to music. I was unable to work during these two-week periods because my concentration was so poor. Crying would start crossing my mind toward the end of two weeks. Suicide would also start crossing my mind at the end of two weeks, partly because I thought this important drug trial had failed and partly because suicidal thoughts are a symptom of depression itself. I would then switch back to antidepressant Asendin. It was too bad because antidepressants can suddenly start working the sixth week. Dr. Haglund had failed to mention this fact about six weeks. That was extremely poor medical practice, in my opinion. The hope for what could happen over the course of an additional four weeks could have kept me going until one of these drugs kicked in.

I told my manager at Dave's Pizza that I had to quit, due to inevitable poor concentration and irritability. I told him that I had manic depression. I had worked there six months and hadn't told him yet. The poor concentration had already set in. I knew I had to quit, or eventually I would be fired because of the poor concentration.

I waited for antidepressant Norpramine to work.

Chapter 25

Finally Trying Antidepressants for Six Weeks

I tried antidepressant Norpramine and a great thing happened. I found I could stand being depressed for more than two weeks without committing suicide. Actually, I had had depression untreated for years before without committing suicide, but in recent years I had thought about suicide after just two weeks without antidepressant Asendin. Suicide crossed my mind the first thirty-nine days on Norpramine, but not after that. Norpramine kicked in suddenly on the fortieth day. I felt less depressed than during the first thirty-nine days. The fortieth day and beyond, I had more energy, I was more optimistic, I had better concentration, and I didn't feel like crying. I woke up the morning of the fortieth day feeling much better.

Antidepressant Norpramine helped a lot, but I was still somewhat depressed. However, Norpramine did not have nearly the side effect problem that antidepressant Asendin did. With less of a low-interest-in-romance side effect, all women looked better all day.

One day a manic depressive named Paul Crosby walked into the WDMDA office. I knew him from a year earlier when he had been on the board of WDMDA. He was a friendly, undepressed kind of guy. He asked me if I was on Social Security disability. I said no and that I thought I had to be broke to be on it. I had some savings from money my dad had given all us kids in the past. Paul said that you just have to be disabled; you don't have to be broke. That was useful information. Paul also asked if I knew Kenneth Boreen. Kenneth Boreen was a corporate raider. Back in the 1980s, corporate raiders made a lot of money by buying a lot of stock in companies and re-organizing them for profit.

I said, "Actually I may have met him at my father's wedding because my father did some business with him."

Kenneth Boreen's mother had been manic depressive, and he knew that I was manic depressive because my dad had told him. Paul Crosby would play a key role in my next manic episode. In my imagination, so would Kenneth Boreen.

After a few months of tricyclic antidepressant Norpramine, I stopped it on July 11. Now, in my battle to be healthy, I was going to try the dangerous monoamine oxidase inhibitor (MAOI) antidepressant Nardil. Dr. Haglund had been bugging me for two years to try an MAOI, but I had always refused because I thought they were too dangerous. Because Norpramine was a tricyclic antidepressant and Nardil was an MAOI antidepressant, it was safest to wait up to two weeks on no drug at all before switching from one to the other. It can be fatal to mix an MAOI with a tricyclic. I, with good reason, was afraid that mixing the two drugs would kill me. I made Dr. Haglund sign a contract that said if I got suicidal, I could be put in the locked psychiatric ward and left there until it was safe to go back on Norpramine. That would be in case of feeling suicidal while having Nardil in my system. Also, the contract said I would not be given electroshock. Electroshock is a last resort treatment for depression, but it causes memory loss. I sent a copy of that contract to a commitment defense lawyer.

I also memorized the list of foods you can't eat while on antidepressant Nardil. There is a long list of common foods that if you eat while on Nardil, you are fairly likely to have a stroke and die. The stroke can happen within an hour of eating these foods. The foods are cheese, pepperoni, yogurt, bananas, raisins, caffeine, chocolate, and alcohol among many others. If you can get to an emergency room fast enough upon getting a headache, the warning sign of the stroke, you will live. Otherwise, you could die or be badly brain damaged.

Dr. Haglund had always said that the waiting period between the two medications was really unnecessary, so on July 15, I started antidepressant Nardil. I had gotten Dr. Haglund to say that this was her idea for me to try this drug and that she would take the blame if anything went wrong. We had taken many precautions. One precaution we hadn't taken was to make a plan for what we would do if I got manic.

CHAPTER 26

MANIC LAWSUIT AIDED BY SECRET AGENTS

The first couple of weeks on antidepressant Nardil, I got a slight lift in my mood and a stimulant side effect, so I couldn't sleep very well. I had to take the sleeping pill Halcion to get to sleep. I still didn't sleep very much, so I experienced what I called the "wired but tired" effect. This is the feeling of being very tired and wanting to sleep, but having too much stimulant in you to fall asleep. It would be similar to a normal person who pushes himself to stay up late and get little sleep and takes a lot of caffeine to stay awake. It is a very weird feeling and gives you poor concentration and energy. I continued to go to the WDMDA office and answer phones. We didn't get much done there, but we played a mean game of phone tag.

On August 2, 1988, my brother Steve, my brother Johnny, and my niece Dana arrived from Israel. Steve and Dana lived there, and Johnny was visiting. My sister-in-law Amy would be coming in a couple weeks. Our house would be full for a while.

I was feeling very excited and optimistic. I bought a *Wall Street Journal*. I saw Dr. Haglund later that day, and she was afraid I might be getting manic because I was laughing more than usual. Reading

The Wall Street Journal was also a sign that I was getting manic because manic people often plan on being big business tycoons. Dr. Haglund gave me the name of Dr. Harry Dellwo to call in case she was out of town.

On about August 3, I started flexing my hands alternately as if I were swimming freestyle, or I would flex them together as if I was swimming butterfly. It was a very exciting feeling. Feeling this good reminded me of when I had been healthy and had been swimming. I thought about my old teammates and our meets. It was very pleasant—much better than depression.

On August 5, I went car shopping with my cousin Laura Felber. I couldn't stop laughing. It was so much fun. Car salesmen were so funny. One tried to sell her rust proofing plus fabric protection for one thousand dollars. Rustproofing should sell for about three hundred dollars, so she would be getting seven hundred dollars worth of Scotchguard for her seats. I thought that was hysterical.

Also, we went to a Honda dealer who said, "Because Hondas are imported, we only get X amount."

Laura said later that the term "X amount" had been used in a movie starring comedian Steve Martin, and it was a big joke because Steve had thought "X" really meant something specific, rather than being a variable.

When she said, "It was from a Steve Martin movie." I just couldn't stop laughing. I laughed for about twenty minutes straight. I really did.

I was optimistic because I hadn't laughed that much in years. During this time, I was writing e-mail letters to Dave Frish, my old poker friend, and I told him all about the new drug. I finally sent him a funny letter that talked about the sprinkling bans that were in effect. I told him that if you violate the sprinkling ban, they fly over your house spraying Agent Orange. Then your grass won't be green for a long,

long time. Agent Orange was a defoliant used to kill vegetation in the Vietnam War.

By August 6, my dad was starting to get concerned about me. He heard my hysterical laughter and started to think I was getting manic.

On the morning of the seventh, I babysat Dana, my niece. I carried her around the house singing "Twist and Shout" and other Beatles songs. I said to people later, "The more Beatles you teach them now, the less you have to teach them later."

My concentration was very poor. I was busy thinking so much of funny or successful things to say in the future that I was not paying attention to the present. I was manic, but I didn't recognize it in myself. This was mostly because people in the manic phase don't usually recognize their own mania, and also because in my previous manias, I didn't laugh so much. I was sure it couldn't be mania because of the laughter. I also was sleeping only about four or five hours a night because of the drug. I couldn't pay attention to dinner table conversation since my concentration was so poor. I just stared into space thinking funny thoughts. Everyone else was eating, but I ate much more slowly than they did because I was so distracted.

On the ninth, I called Dr. Haglund and asked permission to take less antidepressant Nardil. It was the first time in my life that I wanted to take less of an antidepressant.

Dr. Haglund agreed that that would be a good idea.

On the tenth, I had an appointment with Dr. Haglund. I came about twenty minutes late, instead of the usual ten minutes early. This was because I was laughing so hard that I left the house late, and then I missed the exit off the freeway. This again was because I was too busy thinking about funny things. Dr. Haglund said I was manic and should start mood leveler lithium. I said in a very angry voice that lithium makes all my muscles twitch. She never seemed to listen to me say that in the past. Then she said that I should try the antipsychotic Mellaril to treat my mania.

I said angrily, "Dr. Haglund, do you read your own literature?" (I read lots of literature, including some written by her.) This was because Dr. Haglund had come out with some literature saying that antidepressants are for depression, while the drugs usually grouped with Mellaril (antipsychotics) were for mania. I didn't think I was manic.

Dr. Haglund had sometimes prescribed the antipsychotic Mellaril for depression, in apparent contradiction to her own writing. I felt she was misprescribing Mellaril again. This time she was right; she was prescribing it for mania, but I felt I was still depressed. I didn't think I was manic. In spite of the laughter, I still thought I was in the depressed phase. I was out of touch with reality. Dr. Haglund brought in Dr. Dellwo for a minute to see me, and when he saw me laughing, he started naming drugs I should have. I refused all medication changes except to quit the antidepressant Nardil and agreed to come and see Dr. Dellwo on Friday the twelfth. Dr. Haglund would be out of town.

On August 11, I called Dr. Haglund in the morning and asked her, "Will this be a new chapter in a psychiatry textbook?"

She said, "No. It's just hypomania." (Hypomania means a little bit of mania.)

I said, "Good guess."

I felt this was a new phenomenon because I had never laughed so much during mania, and I had never heard of a situation where anyone laughed so much. It annoyed me greatly to have Dr. Haglund say I was manic because I knew that meant she wanted me to go into the hospital, which would be no fun. I was having fun on the outside, and I felt the drugs for mania would bring me down to a deep depression. I felt they would turn me into a zombie, like some of the people at the WDMDA support group meetings who were on antipsychotics, even though they didn't need them at such a high dose. I thought antidepressant Nardil would just wear off in two weeks and I would be okay.

The next day I went to see Dr. Dellwo. Diane Estenson, my cousin by marriage, had told me not to drive while laughing constantly, so I took a cab. I told the cab driver to drive anywhere on campus that would sell a small portable tape player. I was going to record the session with Dellwo, so if he said anything wrong I could sue him.

I got to one of the drugstores on the UW campus and hurriedly bought a tape recorder, batteries, and tapes. I then ran to the University Hospitals building where Dr. Dellwo has his office. I hoped that he would just give me some more of the sleeping pill Dalmane. I thought that just some Dalmane to get me sleeping eight hours again— along with the wearing off of the stimulant and antidepressant Nardil—would make me okay. I was expecting, though, that Dr. Dellwo would say I was manic, so the tape would be evidence of malpractice. I didn't think he should call me manic, when I was sure it was just too much antidepressant Nardil lifting up my mood.

I later summarized my visit with Dr. Dellwo in a letter to Randy Harold who I knew from University of Puget Sound but hadn't talked to in six years. I also sent the letter to Phil Holland. Phil was one of my Mercer Island poker buddies. Both were lawyers, but by sending letters to them, I was showing the symptom of excessive letter writing, which comes with mania. Here is how I summarized my meeting with Dr. Dellwo in the letters. The unbracketed parts are part of the original letter. The symbols "()" also show part of the original letter. The symbols "[]" show my notes added here for clarity:

Enter Bill: (tape rolling visibly) I say, "This is Bill Hannon, manic-depressive as usual.' (Assumes immediate misdiagnosis of mania, assumes correctly, and we know manic people don't think they're sick.)

[Let me explain. I had the tape recorder rolling. I was expecting to be called manic. I didn't think I was manic. I meant that if I were manic, I wouldn't even go to a doctor. Manics generally don't go to a doctor. Manics are generally irresponsible. I was doing something responsible by going to a doctor. I thought that if I were really manic, I would not be at the doctor's office. Given that I was there, I must be healthy. Kind of like the novel *Catch 22*.]

Dr. Dellwo: "You're manic." (Basically insane.)

Bill: "It's just too much Nardil!" [Too much Nardil was the best name for my diagnosis that day, I thought.]

Dr. Dellwo: (Asking someone he judges insane for their own medical history.) "How much Nardil are you taking?"

Bill: "What did it say on my chart?"

Dr. Dellwo: "I don't have your chart. I've never seen it, and medical records are totally irrelevant to the practice of medicine anyway." [Actually he said they were not always necessary to medical practice because he could just look at me. I was clearly in a manic state, given that he knew a little of my history from talking to Dr. Haglund.]

Bill: "Sounds like malpractice already."

Dr. Dellwo: "Let's go have a look at the locked psychiatric ward."

What does this sound like to you?

I meant at the time that I wrote the letter that it sounded like malpractice. It seemed like he would want to put me in there and dope me up and take the tape recorder to destroy the evidence that he didn't have my chart. A week later, I inflated my fears to the paranoid level that he wanted to put me in the hospital and deliberately overdose me and kill me, to shut me up forever.

I still have the tape of that visit. Being in the hospital would have been right. I told him I wasn't sleeping much and was laughing all day.

I told him one thing I was laughing about: the training program for Dave's Pizza drivers. I said, "As soon as you're hired, you get together with upper management and they spend eight hours telling you 'Don't speed, stop at red lights, and don't speed' and so on."

I continued, "When you get to your store, managers won't tell you to speed, but senior drivers will tell you, that you can go forty-five miles per hour down 76th Avenue, no problem. (Seventy-sixth Street is in a thirty-mile-per-hour zone.) The managers can be standing right there, and they just won't say anything. This is the Dave's Pizza Hot Rod Society."

Dr. Dellwo didn't think that was funny.

At the end of the session, I told Dr. Dellwo that he and Dr. Haglund were fired from my case. I told him that Dr. Haglund could call me to get her job back but that Dr. Dellwo could not call me.

Saturday and Sunday August 13 and 14, we were planning to go up to the mountains, but my dad cancelled the trip when I told him that Dr. Dellwo thought I was manic. My dad wanted us to stay near a hospital so I could check into it if necessary. I was planning on staying home so I could be near my WDMDA friends, and my dad wanted to stay home with me and have everybody else go up to the mountains.

I said, "No, if Lee (my father's name is Lee) is home alone, I'm at a friend's house or in a hotel. I'm not staying alone with him!"

So, everybody stayed home. I figured this cancelled camping trip was another part of the damages claim that I could use in my malpractice case against Dr. Haglund and Dr. Dellwo.

My Dad had talked to Dr. Dellwo, and I had told him that Dr. Dellwo thought I was manic, so I thought his misdiagnosis was unnecessarily worrying my dad and the rest of my family. I thought that the obvious answer was for me to stop taking antidepressant Nardil and keep taking the sleeping pill Dalmane. I thought that would straighten me out and we could go to the mountains and have fun, but Dr. Dellwo wouldn't even give me anymore Dalmane. I felt it was Dr. Dellwo's fault that the camping trip was cancelled.

Dr. Dellwo was really right; I was very manic. On the fourteenth, I was home alone. (Everyone else was just out somewhere locally.) The phone rang, and now I'll quote from the letter I wrote to Phil Holland and Randy Harold, who were my lawyer friends in distant cities:

Sunday, I get a phone call that sounds a Hell of a lot like Dr. Dellwo. He said, "Howard Greenberg high school classmate of Lee Hannon calling from Albany, New York." He gave some area code like 518 or 519, which was right for Albany. Then he gave a local number. I called Albany long distance information (a free call) and said, "You got a Howard Greenberg?" A couple of Greenbergs, no Howards, no initial "H." No Greenbergs whose local number matches the one he gave. Talk about annoying telephone calls! It was Dr. Dellwo trying to get through to my dad to tell him that I'm insane, when I'm not! Haven't I had enough trouble getting along with my dad already? I called 911. The Mercer Island police were there in about twenty minutes. They've got his name and they know where he works. Nuisance phone calls! Also, I happen to know that there weren't all that many Jews in Spokane Central Class of '44. If there were, my dad probably didn't hang out with them anyway. He was only slightly Jewish. Actually, Howard Greenberg is a very good Jewish name for a non-Jew to think up. Did names like Noah Aaron Goldstein ring a bell anywhere at the University of Washington? Guess who? It was me.

I was really annoyed. I called to get a trace put on our line like the cop told me to. This was before the days of caller ID. This was so that I could prove that it was really Dr. Dellwo posing as Greenberg.

However, the line was in my father's name, so I needed his permission for the trace. Obviously, that wasn't going to work.

I decided to fight fire with fire. It was Sunday night, so I decided the only part of the hospital that was open was the emergency room. I called there and said, "This is a friend of Noah Aaron Goldstein, and he just got an extremely annoying phone call from what sounds like Dr. Dellwo."

They said, "Oh, really?"

I said, "Yes, so could you take a message?"

"Well, who is the message for?"

"For everyone at the hospital. Just tell them that Dr. Dellwo makes extremely annoying phone calls, and the police have already been notified."

Months later I found out that Howard Greenberg was really Howard Grenberg and was a real person living in Albany, New York. He really was a high school classmate of my dad. He spells his name with only one *e* in the first syllable.

On the fifteenth, I called the information line for Trenton Hospital that they always advertise on the radio. All I knew was that Trenton Hospital had nothing to do with the University Hospitals. It was private and was not a teaching hospital, so I thought I'd have fair odds of getting a good psychiatrist there. All my laughter was fun. It just wasn't practical. I knew that, but I didn't think I was manic. I hadn't laughed so much in previous manic episodes. I wanted a new doctor to prescribe the sleeping pill Dalmane and to testify in my lawsuit against Dr. Haglund and Dr. Dellwo that I was not manic.

That night I walked around a lake with Laura Felber, Diane Estenson, and my brother, Steve. I absolutely could not pay attention to what anyone was saying. I was lost in space. I do remember that the colors seemed so much brighter than they did when I was depressed. The grass seemed intensely green, and the lake intensely blue. In my mind, I was rehearsing testimony for my big lawsuit; that's why I couldn't pay attention to the conversation. Later, Kevin Felber joined us, and I told him some Dave's Pizza jokes, like: When does a Dave's Pizza chef wash his hands? Only after making an anchovy pizza or when he's getting ready to go home. I thought that was very funny, and it was true.

On the sixteenth, I called some local malpractice lawyers. They said they'd call me back. That night I took some hay fever drug Benadryl to help me sleep. It is for hay fever and has a drowsiness side effect. It is the only hay fever drug you can take by mouth when antidepressant Nardil is still in you. I had run out of sleeping medication, so I had to take the Benadryl for the drowsiness. I still knew I should be sleeping, and that would eventually save me. I was in possession of some mood leveler lithium, and that had a drowsiness side effect. However, taking lithium could be construed as a treatment for mania. Therefore, I didn't want to take lithium, because if I got better by taking it, that would suggest that I was manic, and my lawsuit hinged on the idea that I was not manic.

I was talking on the phone every day to my manic depressive friend Paul Crosby. He really didn't like his previous doctors, and was glad I was planning to sue some.

I was also talking to my healthy friend Howard Schultz. He knew I was not normal because of all the laughter, and he thought I was paranoid. He was right. I was paranoid.

Being manic feels really good. I was getting intense feelings, which reminded me very vividly of being back in eleventh and the first part of twelfth grade. Those times were fun and had really been the best times of my life. I started thinking a lot about Melanie Carson. In my five-page letter to the lawyers, Randy Harold, and Phil Holland, I mentioned that I had been out cutting the grass with no shirt and no suntan lotion. I said that I came in and got a glass of orange juice and noticed something in the paper about fewer babies being born in May because of the heat in August. This article reminded me to put on some sunscreen. The whole thing was reminding me of my high school senior class trip to Jamaica, where I got to know Melanie Carson and where I got a massive sunburn. This time, at least, I didn't get sunburned. The memories were intense, even though Jamaica had been eleven years earlier. It was fun and exciting.

I also continued alternately flexing my hands like I was swimming freestyle or simultaneously like I was swimming butterfly. It reminded me of summer camp in 1976.

On the seventeenth, I was watching the news. They said the Hispanic FBI had walked off the job. This fact has to do with law enforcement, which meshes with my idea that the world needs to be saved from crime. A month earlier, also on the news, it was reported that in North Miami Beach, gangs of teenagers was grabbing women up off the beach in broad daylight and raping them. People would just stand there and watch, afraid to do anything. None of the perpetrators was ever arrested. I had been thinking that in my testimony at the malpractice trial of Dr. Haglund and Dr. Dellwo, I would say what it was like to be really manic and obsessed with fighting crime. I would talk about my delusions during my mania of 1980 and 1981—that I could save the world from crimes like these. I knew I had been manic then; I just didn't think I was manic currently.

On the eighteenth, my brother Steve's friend, Scott, was over at our house. Steve and Scott were talking in our living room and I was across the room. I picked up *The Seattle Jewish World* (a weekly newspaper) and Scott turned to me quite suddenly and said, "There is nothing for you in *The Jewish World* this week."

Then Scott's six-year-old daughter repeated, "There is nothing for you in *The Jewish World*."

I found it odd that Scott interrupted himself to say that. One thing about Scott was that he had the same job that Melanie Carson did. He was a surgical nurse. I thought there was a big conspiracy tying Scott, Melanie, myself, and dozens of others together to help me win my lawsuit. It was a delusion of grandeur. I opened *The Seattle Jewish World* to the only section I always read, the section on weddings, births, and deaths. There it was: a death notice for Lee Gross of North Miami Beach. This notice had to be fake for several reasons. Lee was my dad's first name. Hadn't I been saying that he had been gross for years in the past? I thought it was a secret clue to me from the FBI. I thought they would know that I had only heard of North Miami Beach in the context of crime. Also, who in Seattle would care about someone in North Miami Beach? I knew then that enough people had heard about my situation so that they were trying to help me by putting secret clues in the newspapers. The "Death of Lee Gross" obituary was a secret clue. *There was really no such person,* I thought. The FBI was just trying to encourage me by giving this clue.

In my delusions, I figured that the malpractice trial would be a big enough media event that I could say, "Build prisons and keep them full," on the witness stand, in the context of the malpractice trial, and it would make national news. It was very exciting. I was crazy, but I didn't know it. I was having fun. It was great having a sense of purpose.

I decided that there was a giant conspiracy of people getting together to try to help me win my malpractice case. It would be a big case because Dr. Haglund and Dr. Dellwo were professors of psychiatry at a university. I decided that the help I was getting was being financed by Kenneth Boreen, the corporate raider friend of my dad. He was being assisted by the FBI and a lot of people who knew me. The phones were tapped, the house was bugged, I was being followed, and my letters were being read—I was sure. This was all in an effort to help me, to know what clues to leave for me, and to know how I would react to certain things. It was all secret, so people would not know that the FBI was helping, I thought. This was a laugh riot. I thought this was great. This was certainly the euphoria and grandiose delusion symptom of mania. Also, when manic, people think they are going to be rich, so that was another symptom. I thought I would get rich from my lawsuit.

Also on the eighteenth, when I sent the letter to my old friends who were now lawyers, Phil Holland and Randy Harold, I included something that alluded to the fact that I thought that the newspaper column "Dear Abby" was aimed directly at me. There was something in "Dear Abby" about defamation of character. I decided this meant I should try not to cut down anybody unnecessarily in my testimony for my lawsuit. It would've involved taking the Fifth Amendment a lot, I thought. Now I understand that just saying something negative about someone is not necessarily a crime. You can say anything that is true. By putting these things in my letters to Harold and Holland, I thought I was confirming that I read "Dear Abby" every day. If they were a part of the secret conspiracy helping me, they would need that information. At this point, I was through writing to Dave Frish. He kept writing back, calling me manic, so I was angry with him. The letter was originally intended for him also, but then I decided the letter contained so much anger toward him that it was better to just let Randy and Phil read it.

On the nineteenth, I had an appointment with a new psychiatrist, Dr. Ken Stark, at Trenton Hospital. My cousin, Laura Felber, drove me there because I still wasn't driving. I told her that she should come in and talk to my shrink with me so that the shrink could gain more information that I might forget to give him. We headed toward the hospital early because there were some stops Laura wanted to make.

First we stopped at a temple where Laura was teaching Sunday school in the fall. She was to meet with a rabbi there.

Laura introduced me to the rabbi, and he said something like, "I have to have a meeting with Laura."

I said, "Speak it in Spanish."

To me these were code words in honor of the Hispanic FBI that had walked off the job (as I had seen in the news) and in honor of the first psychiatrist I had in Israel whose first language was Spanish because he was from Mexico.

Laura and the rabbi went into the office for a meeting, and I sat out in the hall right under the fire alarm. I thought, *When in a Jewish temple, act like a Jew.* Always assume that someone is about to come burn the temple down. Always have Holocaust paranoia if you are acting like a Jew. To me it is "Holocaust paranoia" when American Jews say that there could be a Holocaust in the United States. This very unfairly insults America. I thought, *Pretend to have Holocaust paranoia.* Don't pray; just sit by the fire alarm. So I sat there, and when anybody walked by me, I stood up and got my hands ready to hit the alarm if they tried anything funny. It was a fun game. As people were walking by I said, "Hello." I did this to show I was not truly paranoid. I was just spoofing Holocaust paranoia.

A young woman walked by and I said, "Hi, what's your name?"

She said, "Stacy, what's yours?"

"Bill," I said. "Well, maybe I'll see you around here."

"I doubt it," she said. "Where are you from?"

"Mercer Island,"

"Oh that's good. Bye."

In my delusions, I decided she was an FBI agent sent to follow me. I was trying to be flirtatious. I thought that was the best I could do to encourage the secret private investigators and FBI agents helping me.

After playing the fire alarm game for a while, I walked around the temple looking at the art and other displays.

Laura got done with her meeting, and then we went to a frozen yogurt place. We sat outside, and there was a man with dark sunglasses sitting behind me, alone. Clearly, he was FBI. In order to clue him in that I was picking up my clues, I started to mention to Laura the story about the gang rapes in North Miami Beach. As soon as I said rapes, he belched. I decided that burping was now a signal.

We went to see my new doctor, Dr. Stark. I was in there mostly myself giving my medical history in a hyper tone of voice. I also told him that I thought Dr. Dellwo and Dr. Haglund had motives to kill me right now because I was going to ruin their career by suing them for malpractice. I told him that I had the tape of Dr. Dellwo calling me manic for no reason. I told Dr. Stark that I was not manic, that they were calling me manic, and that this was the basis of the suit.

Dr. Stark also decided I was manic and told me to go back to Dr. Haglund. I told him that Dr. Haglund was out of town, so he said, "Go back to Dr. Dellwo."

I told him, "Dr. Dellwo really wants to kill me."

So, Dr. Stark said, "Well then I'd like to put you in the hospital here and treat you for mania."

I said, "No, could I just have some sleeping medication Dalmane?" He said, "No."

"Well, I don't want to go in the hospital, because you're misdiagnosing me also. I haven't displayed any symptoms of mania here."

"Well, I can't treat you then."

"Okay," I said. "I hope this works out for both of us." We shook hands, and I left. He talked to Laura for a minute, and then we left.

Then Laura said, "You need counseling."

I thought, *Yeah, wouldn't that be funny, and it would appease my family*

a little bit. A psychologist for manic depression and no psychiatrist—
what a laugh. I believed then that psychologists were not good for manic
depression. I thought psychologists should always refer their manic
depressive patients to psychiatrists. Psychologists often did not revere
the medication as much as they should. Back then they did not usually
even understand manic depression.

As I write this in 2017, I now know that many psychologists are not
anti-medication, and so they can help manic depressives. Psychiatrists
and psychologists can cooperate with each other. Manic depressives can
benefit from medication and talk therapy, both.

My family was worried about me, so at least I'd be seeing someone by
seeing a psychologist. That way I could see a mental health professional
until the MAOI antidepressant Nardil wore off. I felt that my family
had some undue faith in psychologists, so if I saw one, they wouldn't
worry or scream as much as they would if I saw nobody. Once the
dangerous Nardil wore off, I would be safely depressed again. I could
go on a safe tricyclic antidepressant. That's what I thought.

I said to Laura, "Yeah, I'll go to a psychologist. Which one?"

She said, "They probably have some here."

So, we turned back around and made an appointment for the twenty-
fourth with a psychologist named Brad Maiers who worked in the same
office as Dr. Stark.

You see, I knew I was not well. I had made up a name for what I
had. It was P.O.M.E.L-N.E.S., "Phenomena of Much Extra Laughter
and Not Enough Sleep." I thought this was different from being manic.
In my other manic episodes, I hadn't laughed so much. Somehow I
didn't equate laughter with the euphoria symptom of mania. I didn't
want the treatment for mania, because I felt I had something different.
I felt it was just too much antidepressant Nardil causing Pomelnes. The
antipsychotics, which are the treatment for mania, would just make my

concentration worse, I felt. Actually, they would have really helped. They do interfere with the concentration of normal people or depressed people. Of course, I was neither.

As Laura and I walked to her car, two people walked by us and one said to the other, "I was listening to Suzanne Vega …"

I figured that he was another FBI agent giving me the clue that my tape of malpractice by Dr. Dellwo was valuable, just like tapes by the singer Suzanne Vega. She had a hit song named "Luka" about child abuse, which is a crime that often goes unreported. Mistakes by psychiatrists also are often unreported. It is the duty of the good doctors to help testify against the bad doctors.

I was feeling very excited and mostly happy. Most hours of the day my happy, grandiose delusion of looking forward to the lawsuit outweighed my paranoid delusion that Dr. Dellwo and Dr. Haglund wanted to kill me. I was extremely glad the FBI wanted to help me with my lawsuit. This excitement was causing me to sleep only three hours per night, but I didn't mind. I didn't feel tired. I was looking forward to the lawsuit very much and was enjoying the thought that I'd be rich. By this time, my fear of being killed was less than it had been.

At the dinner table that night, my sister-in-law Amy was talking about the hassle and red tape they were running into in trying to get a new passport to get Dana back out of the country with them. She was a year old, and they made babies get a new passport each year. They were talking about how some piece of paper had to be mailed from somewhere and stuff like that because Dana was adopted. Amy said that she felt like she was being forced to stay in the country. She said it was like the movie *The Sound of Music*, where the lead man is being forced to stay in Austria because he is being drafted into the Nazi navy. Amy and Steve were going to a play that night.

Amy said, "We could walk out at intermission like they did in *The Sound of Music.*

To me this passport red tape was part of the conspiracy to help me. If they were forced to stay longer, they would be around to help stop my dad from getting me committed, so I could be killed. My dad didn't want to kill me, but he didn't realize that Dr. Haglund and Dr. Dellwo did, I felt. Amy and Steve, I thought, did not think I was as committable or as sick.

Manic people like rhymes and puns. After dinner that night I went into our computer room and the windows were open. Amy and her brother Aaron (who was also visiting) were in there and I said, "I think there's a draft in here." I meant a navy draft and a wind draft.

Amy said, "Okay." I don't know if she understood the pun.

Later that night, my dad came into my bedroom and said—in what seemed like a overbearing voice—"Howard Grenberg just called."

I said, "There is no such person! Get out of my room."

Like I said before, much later I found out that there is a Grenberg, but there is no Greenberg. There is a difference by one *e*.

My dad then took another step into my room and said, "Let's talk privately."

I then screamed, "You don't have the right to talk to me without witnesses!" I then left my room.

He came out of my room and screamed, "Keep your voice down!"

I then yelled, "You don't have the right to talk to me without witnesses!"

He screamed, "Keep your voice down!"

"You shut up totally, and I'll keep my voice down!"

I didn't feel that it was safe to be at my house. I walked away from our house carrying my tape recorder with "Luka" by Suzanne Vega playing loud enough for our neighbors to hear. A song about unreported crimes was appropriate to praise the crime fighting of the FBI. My dad wanted to put me in the hospital with Dr. Dellwo alias Greenberg, I thought. My dad wanted to help me, but I thought he didn't know that Dr. Dellwo would kill me.

With "Luka" playing, it would be a clear enough signal to the private investigators and FBI what I was doing. When I got far enough away, I switched to "Parents Just Don't Understand," a rap song by D.J. Jazzy Jeff and the Fresh Prince. I went to a hotel about a mile from my house, but it was closed. Then I went to a convenience store and called 911 again to report what I thought was a nuisance phone call. I meant the call to my father earlier that evening from Howard Grenberg. I thought it was Dr. Dellwo saying he was Greenberg. The 911 people said that it was no longer a police matter.

I told 911, "I am a mentally ill person. Could you give me a ride to a hotel?"

They said, "No. We don't give people rides. Call a cab."

I called a cab, and when I was out by the street waiting for a cab to go to a hotel downtown, somebody on a three-wheeled moped drove by playing a rap tape. I thought this was a clue from the FBI that they liked my taste in music.

Also, as I was waiting for the cab, somebody lit a firecracker behind the convenience store. I didn't flinch. I thought the secret agents wanted to see if I would flinch.

The cab pulled up, and I hopped in. I told him to go to the Holiday Inn downtown. He said, "Sure."

There was another passenger also in the cab going downtown.

I asked, "Where are you going?"

He said, "I'm going to the bottom of the Davis Street Bridge." I decided this was a suicidal tendency check.

My antidepressant Nardil was wearing off, so they were checking for suicidal thoughts. I calmly asked, "Why are you going to the bottom of the Davis Street Bridge?"

He said, "Well, from there it's just a short walk to where I'm going."

I said, "Okay." I thought he was either joking, or I didn't know the layout of the bridge. At least I didn't have to talk this guy out of a suicide attempt. If he was being facetious, then he was FBI checking on me for a reaction to see if I was suicidal. I left it at that and changed the subject.

Months later I learned that the Davis Street Bridge slopes downhill.

I got to the hotel and checked in. I had a credit card that my dad usually paid off. I felt it was an ordinary hotel room, but the cable channels on the television were numbered unusually, so I thought that they would be playing shows and commercials specifically altered to give secret messages to me. One commercial about fixing up houses got to me. It made me think about possibly buying a house.

I didn't sleep that night, but I lay awake in bed for about four hours, thinking how much fun this was, and I really thought it was a fun adventure. I was in a very good mood. Then I got up, took a shower, and left the hotel. I went down and had some breakfast at a restaurant. I was sure the other customers in the restaurant were some good guys there to watch me.

I placed my order by saying, "Four eggs *scrambled* and four glasses of orange juice." The reason I emphasized the word "scrambled" was to signify to anyone listening that I knew that I had to unscramble the clues coming off the television set and elsewhere. This was a riot.

Then, I went shopping downtown. I thought it would be funny if I worried my family just enough for them to notice that I was gone and not know where I was. I thought this was appropriate because they didn't really listen to me about manic depression. I thought maybe if I just showed up at 10:00 a.m. seeming just fine, they would listen to me when I told them I was all right. I shopped and bought some things, all of which had some symbolic meaning. I bought a shirt that was close to my high school colors. There were shirts exactly my high school colors, but all they had was mediums, the size I wore in high school. I now needed an extra-large because I was so fat. The whole time I thought the stores had been prepared for my shopping trip. The colors were a little off to fit me because high school was a long time ago. I was thinking intensely of high school because I felt good like I had in high school. Some thoughts of the present were mixed in. I went to a science museum and bought a book about the Plains Indians eating buffalo. This was to show the vegetarians in my family, Rick and all the Felbers, that eating meat is natural. They always gave me a hard time and said that I was depressed because I ate hamburgers. I thought they were out of touch with reality. There were little messages I was supposed to pick up in each store, I thought. These messages made it clear that the secret agents helping me had researched me carefully by talking to a lot of people who knew me in the past or present. These were questions like, "Is this book for you?"

To me this was a secret message that I shouldn't be too hard on Rick and the Felbers when I presented them with the buffalo book. Now I realize they were asking if the book was for me as opposed to being for a little kid.

I got home around ten in the morning in a cab, and nobody had noticed I was gone.

That night, in order to get my father further off my case, I called up three of his friends and told them what I thought was going on. I told them, "I think my psychiatrists want to kill me. I know that sounds paranoid, but it could also be true. They gave me a drug that makes me kind of hyper and makes me laugh, so suddenly they diagnose me as manic and say I should be in the hospital. This worries my father, makes him hard to live with, and going into the hospital would mean three weeks racking up a big bill for nothing. Because of the doctor's mistakes, I want to sue the doctors, so now they want to kill me. My dad wants to help me, but he doesn't know that the doctors are out to get me. Also, keep me out of the University Hospitals. If I'm sick, get me to Trenton Hospital."

They mostly just listened and tried to agree with me. A couple of them were going to be at a birthday party for Dana the next day. Overall at this time, when I wasn't feeling paranoid, I was feeling good. I was feeling good most of the day. It reminded me of swimming in high school. Sunday, August 21, 1988 was the birthday party for Dana. My parents invited a bunch of their friends, including some that I had called. They spoke to me, saying things that I thought were supposed to be clues. One of them said something very direct. He said his wife and her twin both work at Trenton Hospital. That was reassuring.

I was still talking to my manic depressive friend Paul Crosby. I was now sure that he was my direct FBI contact. He burped periodically, and I starting thinking that was a clue for emphasis. He denied being in the FBI, but I thought that was part of his job. We talked for a long time. I forget all that we said. A couple times he mentioned that I should do the crossword puzzles in the paper. I thought nothing of it, and I didn't do them.

I was still talking to Howard Schultz every day. I kept telling him that I would be okay in a few days when the antidepressant Nardil wore off.

The next day, I was able to watch the news without laughing. I do remember, however, that on the television show *The Dating Game* I figured the bachelor who won was supposed to be playing the part of me. Imagine! A *Dating Game* show just for me!

On the twenty-fourth, the fourteen days since I had quit

antidepressant Nardil were up, so I started driving again. I also quit eating the restricted diet for Nardil.

Too bad I was still manic.

Now that I was driving, wherever I went, I kept noticing tons of young, half-Asian women. Melanie Carson was half-Asian.

That week, I saw the psychologist Brad Maiers for an hour and he let me tape record the session. His conclusion was that I should also see Dr. Stark and take the medication that he prescribed. So, then I made an appointment to see Dr. Stark.

One night, a bunch of my family was going to rent a video and watch it. I decided to go out to Ted Anderson's house and see if he was home. He was my manic depressive friend who I played Monopoly with sometimes. He wasn't home, so I decided I wanted a night on the town. I figured I'd be feeling good for a while, so I would simulate a date. I wouldn't tell my family where I was going. I'd stay out all night, and come home mid-morning. I drove to a hotel and asked for a room.

The desk clerk looked Hispanic, and I thought that he was working there to say I was right for telling my cousin Laura to speak to the rabbi in Spanish.

I said, "Hablo Engles?"

He said, "Yes."

I said, "Good. Can I have a room?"

"Sure."

He gave me a room. Before I went up to the room, I stopped and looked at the pool for a while. It had a calm, relaxing effect. It reminded me of my old friend, Bridget, who used to check the identification of people going to the university pool.

My mood continued to be happy most of the time. Still, there is a difference between excited happy, and relaxed happy. The pool helped.

I went up to the room and tried to go to sleep. I didn't sleep that much. Instead I just lay there and made plans for my big malpractice lawsuit.

I got up in the morning and bought a newspaper. I walked to a McDonalds for breakfast. The articles in the paper made me laugh. I thought it was printed especially for me, for my entertainment. I was laughing so hard in the McDonald's that I had to throw the newspaper away so that I didn't cause a scene. I was wary about doing anything unusual in public because I didn't want to get arrested, be declared a danger to others or to myself, and put in a psychiatric ward. If I received any treatment for mania, it would ruin my lawsuit.

I took the bus back home. (I had loaned my car to my brother, Johnny, the night before.) My stepmother was quite annoyed with me for not saying where I had been. My brother, Steve, was also upset with me.

Later that day my brother, Johnny, asked me if he could come look in my closet for shirts of his. He looked and didn't find any. Then I looked in his dresser for my clothes and found—where I knew a bunch of my T-shirts were—two of my old Camp Okransky T-shirts. They had sentimental value and had been missing for years, I thought. Now they were back. I decided my friends and relatives had a big game of taking my T-shirts on long trips. I thought they figured that if Bill doesn't get around, at least his T-shirts will. I figured these shirts had been to Israel, Europe, and the Soviet Union because relatives of mine had been there. Now that I was feeling good, they brought all my T-shirts back. It was so much fun.

That evening, we were getting ready to have a Sabbath dinner, but then my dad started talking to me in an angry tone, so I left in my car and went to another hotel. I told Laura Felber, who was also at our house, that I would call her and tell her where I went.

It was a Friday night, so I went for a long cruise. I went up and down and all over the metro area. I finally stopped at a hotel downtown and got a room. I was sure I had been followed on my whole drive by the FBI, who would be leaving clues for my big malpractice suit.

When I got to my hotel room, I was sure that it was bugged and that the phone was tapped. I also figured there were hidden cameras looking back at me through the television set. I thought this was all in the scheme by the FBI and other investigators to help me with my lawsuit.

I couldn't sleep. I was too busy thinking funny thoughts in my head. I wanted to go to sleep. I hadn't slept much for four weeks. I turned off the lights. I couldn't figure out how to shut off the television set. I thought of unplugging it, but I decided I was supposed to leave it on for some reason. There were two doors on the front of the television, so I closed them. There was still a crack down the front of the television between the two doors. The room was dark, but light from the television set was still coming through the crack. The light made an array of beams along the ceiling.

I thought the beams were supposed to suggest what to talk about. I started talking about my past love life and lack thereof. I thought an FBI therapist was listening. I sure hoped he would keep this confidential. I kept trying to shut my eyes and go to sleep, but then a bright beam would make me open my eyes again. After great hesitation and talking about everyone else I ever liked first, I finally talked about Melanie Carson, wishing we could both be well and be together. I mentioned everyone I ever had a crush on who I could remember. I tried not to mention people who were married. The beams of light from the television seemed to clue me in on what to say next to the bugged walls. I mentioned one of the girls I liked in 1976 at Camp Okransky when I was well. She was now married and lived in Israel. Her parents still lived in Ballard, which is a part of Seattle. Finally, after all this fantasizing, I slept for a couple of hours.

When I woke up, I turned on the radio. At some point, they mentioned a three-car accident in Ballard. "Three" refers to adultery, a romantic triangle. I thought the radio broadcast had been altered to mention that accident in Ballard, so that I would get confirmation that the walls really were bugged, and I thought they heard me talk about the girl I knew from camp who was married.

Later that day I was at my dad's house and my WDMDA friend Roger Dymoke called and asked me a bunch of questions about how I was doing. He went through the various symptoms of mania, and I pretty much denied most of them.

The conversation about ended there, and I told him I would see my new doctor, Dr. Stark, on Tuesday and that I'd be okay. I guessed Roger was in on the conspiracy to help me with my lawsuit. It was all handled in a way so that people could deny their participation, I guessed, because this was outside of the FBI's usual jurisdiction.

That night I went over from the hotel to my Aunt Brenda Felber's house with Laura Felber and Amy and Steve Hannon. I told Laura that I wished there was a way for me to calm down. I was no longer afraid that Dr. Dellwo would kill me, but I was still nervous about it.

I asked my cousin Laura to give me a backrub, and she did. She gave me a backrub for about an hour. While she was, I was thinking thoughts about my past. I was thinking about my lack of dating since 1979 and that I wanted to date some more. I couldn't exactly make up for lost time, but I sure wanted to try. I thought most people, including Laura, had continuing love lives and it was a whole area of existence that I wanted to start again.

We watched a video of some movie, and then we watched *Saturday Night Live*. I thought some of the *Saturday Night Live* skits were made just for me. I went back to the hotel and slept better because of the back rub.

On Tuesday, I went to international folk dancing. I didn't know many of the dances, so I often sat and read some of the magazines that were in a lounge area near the dance floor. I looked at one of the magazines, and it was addressed to Mercer Island zip code 98040. The "4" had two prongs going straight up, rather than being a closed *4*. I was sure this was a clue to me to read the whole magazine and check for more clues. I went into another room and read most of the magazine. I figured the FBI knew I didn't do many of the dances and often read the magazines. Especially interesting to me were some statistics being used as a joke that included "99 percent." I thought this was supposed to remind me of the time that Melanie Carson was impressed when I told her of my 99th percentile SAT scores. I went back down to the lounge near the dance floor. A woman named Grace who danced with me sometimes came up and asked me to dance. She had long, straight, shiny blonde hair. However, today I thought this was another secret message. A girl I knew from camp in 1976 had long, straight, shiny blonde hair, and my first doctor in Israel also had straight blonde hair. The international folkdance that Grace and I did was choreographed by a guy named *Cansaywho*. I interpreted that as *can't say who*. This meant that Grace couldn't say that the FBI told her to do the dance with me.

One night in my hotel room at the end of the month, I decided that just for that night, I would watch *The Johnny Carson Show* on TV. Melanie Carson had a brother named Johnny, and I had a brother named Johnny. It seemed like the right thing to do.

The next morning, I drove to a small town to check out real estate prices. I didn't get farther than picking up a local newspaper and concluding that all the ads in there were actually secret clues saying that the FBI wasn't ready for me to move out of the hotel yet, so I drove back down to the hotel.

One day, I had another appointment with Dr. Stark. He convinced me that the antipsychotic Thorazine would help me sleep. I had just wanted the sleeping pill Dalmane, but he got me to leave with a prescription for Thorazine, a sedating, calming, delusion-erasing, sleep-inducing, antipsychotic medication—and therefore the treatment for mania. He wanted to put me in the hospital, but I refused. On August 31, I talked to my manic depressive friend and, I thought, secret FBI contact, Paul Crosby. I was laughing about the fact that Dr. Stark was attempting what he called outpatient treatment for mania. If you are manic, you should be in the hospital. I was jumping to the idea that if you are manic, you would be in the hospital. I was out of the hospital, so I must be okay, I thought. I was laughing with Paul about that, and I told him that I hadn't been sleeping much. I hadn't slept for six days.

Paul said, "Look, this is serious now. Take the medication since you haven't been sleeping."

I said, "Really?"

"Yeah."

"Is that an order?"

"Yeah."

So that night I took some antipsychotic Thorazine, and some side effect drug Cogentin, and slept for about six hours.

In my hotel room, I had some manic depression literature. I started reading some of it and decided that the private investigators and FBI had substituted alternate versions of the literature in order to give me certain messages. I threw the changed versions out in the hall to show I had received their message. There was also *The Book of Questions*, which I started writing answers in, and then when I thought the questions were getting too personal, I threw it out in the hall. I thought it was a different version and was part of the scheme to see what I was thinking. I was thinking about Melanie Carson.

One article about depression had a picture on the cover of someone who looked a lot like Karen Piel. She is one of the married women who went to international folk dancing. I decided to get rid of this article also. I didn't want it to look like I was carrying around pictures of married women to whom I was attracted. I didn't want any scandals.

There was also the question of my cassette tapes. I had some with me that were store-bought, and I had some that were recorded off records. I figured the ones recorded off records were taped illegally, and therefore against federal copyright law, and it seemed they kept disappearing. When I left the room, I figured that the people secretly helping me took the pirated tapes as a signal to me that I had to stay law-abiding or they wouldn't help me.

A major issue was that somehow my tape of my session with Dr. Dellwo had apparently been sabotaged. It was wound around itself many different ways, and was off its spool, so I thought Dr. Dellwo had hired someone to wreck it. I still had a copy of it in my dad's house, and I thought the wrecked version could be fixed, so I started carrying around the wrecked original version in my pocket.

I felt better from the antipsychotic Thorazine. I felt calmer, and I slept.

The antipsychotic Thorazine was starting to bring me down from mania, but I still had a long way to go. On the fifth, I finally figured out how to turn off the television in my hotel room. (Hold the button down for a second.) I still didn't think I was manic; I just needed the Thorazine to sleep as a result of the stress of almost being murdered by Dr. Dellwo and Dr. Haglund, I thought. I would get an apartment, apply for welfare, and pursue my lawsuit against Dellwo and Haglund. One law firm had already turned down this medical malpractice case, but they said I had three years to file suit. I would have three years to shop for a lawyer. Overall, my mood remained mostly good. I was optimistic about the lawsuit, and I figured I had told so many people about Dr. Haglund and Dr. Dellwo that they didn't dare do anything to me.

On the sixth, I heard the song on the radio, "Downtown." I thought this was deliberately put on the radio to tell me to go downtown and rent a safety deposit box in which to put my tapes of my session with Dr. Dellwo. So, I went downtown, rented a safety deposit box at a bank, and put the tapes in it. I thought the number of the box they gave me had some special meaning. It was a number like 2004, which was, I guessed, the first year I could reasonably be a grandparent if I got busy right away.

Delusions were still forming with ease. I went from the hotel to stop by my father's house on the sixth, and there was a message for me to call MS Realty. I thought, did this mean call MS reality? I had heard that Melanie Carson had multiple sclerosis, abbreviated "MS." What was the reality part for? Maybe in reality, she didn't have it. Maybe someone just said that to get me to quit thinking about her. Wouldn't that be great? I sent a letter to Phil Holland, one of my distant lawyer and high school classmate friends. The letter included my delusions about Melanie. Phil was also the former boyfriend of a friend of Pattie Kingston. Pattie was now a lawyer and used to be friends with Melanie. I liked writing to lawyers; after all, there were still two people around who wanted to kill me because I was going to sue them and wreck their careers. I also wrote to Melissa Jenkins. Melissa was Melanie's lab partner back in eleventh-grade physics. Melissa was now a lawyer. I mentioned my current situation and made references to Melanie like I was wondering if we could be fixed up. Or was I flipping out? I also wrote to Doug Bossard, my University of Puget Sound friend whom I hadn't seen in years. He used to know Melanie, and in my letter, I wondered if it was true that she had MS.

Early in September, when I came out of the hotel to the parking lot, I noticed something strange on my car. There was a little piece of masking tape on the lower left hand corner of my windshield. Of course, I took it as a sign that meant that my car was bugged and that I was being followed—and I shouldn't have any contraband in my car because it was visible. Also, things could get stolen out of my car, so I should be careful. I decided that I could leave a towel I stole from the hotel in the car because everybody steals towels from hotels and I needed it to wipe the dew off my car in the morning. A little piece of masking tape meant all that.

On the ninth, I was in Seattle, looking for an apartment to rent, and I came to an avenue that ran east and west. In Seattle, the avenues go north and south, and the streets go east and west. I took this as a clue that the FBI had scrambled the street sign in order to tell me not to rent an apartment on that street.

One day when I was at the hotel restaurant, I decided to spoof good nutrition. For lunch, I had a beer and a chocolate malt.

By the thirteenth, the antipsychotic Thorazine was working well enough for me to carry on the conversation necessary to rent an apartment. I didn't think the want ad or the caretaker were using a secret code. I rented an apartment in Kent. I thought that would be a good suburb to live in because it had a low crime rate.

That evening, I rented a truck, and with the help of Kevin Felber, Carl Paige, Jim Eckhart, and Howard Schultz, I moved my furniture from my dad's place to my apartment. I slept there that night.

Also on the fourteenth, I saw the psychiatrist Dr. Stark. I asked for permission to increase the dose of my antipsychotic Thorazine. He said okay. I also told him of my plan to write to the medical licensing boards of all fifty states, the District of Columbia, Guam, Puerto Rico, the U.S. Virgin Islands, and American Samoa to tell them to never let Dr. Haglund or Dr. Dellwo practice there. I had the addresses, and I was working on the letters. Dr. Stark said he wanted to talk to my dad. I assume this was to get my dad to tell me to stop writing the letters. I told Dr. Stark not to, so he didn't.

That week I had applied for Social Security disability. I had to come up with the name, address, and dates worked for every job I ever had. I also had to describe the job and why I left. They said they'd let me know in five months.

I also wrote another letter to Melissa Jenkins, Phil Holland, and Doug Bossard, inquiring about Melanie Carson's health, and asking if we should be fixed up. Or was I having delusions?

I was feeling very good. I could win a big lawsuit and be rich. On September 22, I was talking to my WDMDA friend, Paul Crosby. I also thought he was my secret FBI contact. I talked to him every day. For a while he had been telling me to do the crossword puzzle in the Seattle paper every day. Also for a while, when he burped, I thought that the burping was supposed to be a clue for emphasis. I hadn't really worked on the crossword puzzles, but today he said, "You really have got to do today's crossword puzzle. There are important things you need to know for your life."

I finally caught on: there were clues in the crossword puzzle! I got the paper. It was unbelievable! The answer to one across was "Carson" Paul said, as he burped. The clue was "Johnny namesake," (after the "Tonight Show" host "Johnny Carson") I have a brother Johnny, and so does Melanie Carson. I couldn't stop laughing. There was more in the crossword puzzle. Five across was "Kingston." The clue was "Capitol of Jamaica." Pattie Kingston had been Melanie Carson's roommate on our high school senior class trip to Jamaica. Jamaica was where I got to know Melanie. I was just rolling with laughter. This was too good to be true! I wrote to some distant friends about Melanie, and they got back to me through the crossword puzzle! Was my mail being read by the

FBI? Or was one of my distant friends an agent? How did they get the job of writing the crossword puzzle? The hows and whys didn't matter. It sure worked pretty well. I was ecstatic. I wrote to Melissa Jenkins, Doug Bossard, and Phil Holland again, and asked about Melanie and me. They still have never written back.

Late in September, I saw Dr. Stark. We decided I would switch to the antipsychotic Loxitane ; I thought it might have fewer side effects than antipsychotic Thorazine.

Early in October, there was some candy piled up on the doorway to my apartment building. There is a Jewish tradition of throwing candy at a bride and groom rather than rice. So, I thought the possibility for me to get married was there, according to someone. I thought the implied bride was Melanie. After all, I felt more romantically inclined, now that I was not depressed.

In October, I continued to go to international folk dancing, WDMDA, and a few restaurants. Wherever I went, the women looked much more attractive than when I was depressed. Also, colors seemed brighter. At WDMDA, I got fired from facilitating support groups because I kept telling everybody to sue their doctors.

I went dancing at a bar once. Something I thought may have been a clue was that almost all of the women I danced with that night were named Bonnie or Bonita. Later, I decided that thinking those names were a clue was a manic symptom, so I shouldn't be ridiculous. I decided I should only accept information that was clear.

I anonymously sent the hotel I stayed at ten dollars to pay for the towel I had stolen. I felt that this way in my lawsuit, if I ever was asked the question, "Did you commit any crimes against the hotel?" I could say no. I told Paul Crosby about this, and he started chewing me out for being so honest, so I started to wonder if he really was an FBI agent. I had already made a list of my secret clues that I thought I could prove were messages. If they were really messages, I could win my lawsuit. The basic premise of my lawsuit was that Dr. Dellwo and Dr. Haglund called me manic, even though I was not. My story was that this false diagnosis caused me a lot of problems. As long as these things were clues and not delusions, then I hadn't been manic, and I could win my case.

I told Paul about some of the incidents I have just written about. He said, "They were due to human error and coincidence, not to anyone trying to send you a secret message."

The next day, Paul and I went over the whole list of delusions, and he told me they were just coincidences. I had been manic. Shoot! I was annoyed. I wrote Phil Holland, Doug Bossard, and Melissa Jenkins and told them to kindly disregard my letters.

I finally recognized my delusions as delusions. I finally could separate reality from fantasy. I was near normal. The antipsychotic Thorazine and then the antipsychotic Loxitane had brought me down to normal. Let's hear it for the medication!

Chapter 27

Conclusion 1997

On October 28, 1988, I saw Dr. Stark and said, "I realize that I've been manic."

He said, "Well, I think that's a major breakthrough."

I continued the antipsychotic Loxitane for several months.

I learned from my last manic episode to take a tape recorder to every psychiatric session. Dr. Stark won't let me record the whole session, but he records a two-minute summary at the end of each session. This will make it easier to sue him in the future if I have to. It's not just my medical history; it is his work history, too.

Speaking of my medical history, it is my memory that we use for my medical history. Dr. Stark has my history written down, but he doesn't know it and never reads it.

I've also started keeping a log book of every time I take a pill. I also write down any change in mood, any change in side effects, and I write down how much I slept.

Dr. Stark was good, but he made one mistake. He left me on the antipsychotic Loxitane, though it causes more low-interest-in romance side effect than antipsychotic Prolixin. I had to ask him which one has the least side effects, and then he told me about Prolixin. I had thought the old fashioned typical antipsychotics were all the same. He should have told me sooner.

By January 1989, my mania went away and I tried just mood leveler lithium by itself with no antipsychotic.

Anyway, mood leveler lithium by itself didn't work for preventing depression. After a few weeks of just lithium, I got depressed. I decided lithium plus an antidepressant should be tried. In the past, lithium plus antidepressant Asendin didn't work very well because that combination made me too drowsy. But there is a rule, if drug A plus drug B doesn't work, that does not rule out drug A plus drug C. It does not rule out drug B plus drug C. It also does not rule out drug A or B by themselves.

So, I tried mood leveler lithium plus antidepressant Wellbutrin. That combination made me manic in four days. However, this time there was a difference. I recognized mania in myself! I had gone to bed at 11 p.m. and was wide awake, lying in bed until 4 a.m. I was thinking happy optimistic thoughts. I was excited about the future. I knew this was the lack of sleep of mania. The antidepressant Wellbutrin lifted my mood up too much. I started myself back on antipsychotic Prolixin, the side effect drug Cogentin, and quit the Wellbutrin and lithium. Cogentin does stop the muscle stiffness and restlessness side effects of Prolixin.

It was a major breakthrough to recognize mania in myself. The lack of sleep was the sign of mania that I could consistently recognize. For a couple years, when I slipped into a depression, I again deliberately induced mania with mood leveler lithium and antidepressant Wellbutrin.

It felt better to be under treatment for mania with antipsychotic Prolixin than it did to be under treatment for depression. By 1991, I was fairly well convinced that being in a controlled mania was more fun than being in a controlled depression.

The combination that worked for a while was antipsychotic Prolixin at bedtime to make me sleep and stop mania, and then, in the morning, side effect drug Cogentin for Prolixin's muscle stiffness side effect. The Cogentin also got rid of some of the main intended sedation effect of Prolixin. So, I was less sedated during the day when I took Cogentin in the morning. I learned from reading *The Handbook of Psychotropic Agents* (Compendium Publications Group, Ltd., of Secaucus, New Jersey) that Cogentin gets rid of some of the main tranquilizing, sedation effect of Prolixin. Reading psychiatry books has helped me a lot. Knowledge is power.

There is a problem with having this prolonged drug-controlled mania. Most of the old-fashioned typical antipsychotics, like Prolixin, that you need to control mania can eventually cause tardive dyskinesia, a strange muscle disease. It causes involuntary movements. I was at risk for that.

I should note that a few lucky manic depressives are controlled fairly well by mood leveler lithium alone. Many hold full-time jobs and have significant others. They don't function fully normally though. Many do function better than I do.

Going back to October 1989, there was a coincidence. One of my friends, Carl Paige, and my barber don't know each other. However, one week in October 1989, they both suggested that I write a book about manic depression. I had been unemployed for a while, collecting Social Security disability and getting some money from my dad. I certainly had time to write a book. I went to a support group meeting and noticed that all the literature there was written by doctors. None of it was written by patients. I figured we needed a book written by a patient. So, I started writing this book. It took many drafts and the help of sixty-five people, but I stuck with it, and this book is the outcome. I joined a writers' group, and that helped a lot.

To support myself, I've been getting Social Security disability, some money from my dad, and some paychecks from part-time jobs. I need my dad's help because I still have trouble holding jobs. I'm very lucky that my dad has had the ability and desire to help me financially. Without his help, I would probably be homeless. I tend to get fired for being too slow. I still have a few side effects of medication and a few symptoms of the disease. I still have poor concentration.

The thing is, now I feel better. Being in a controlled mania feels better than being in a poorly controlled depression. The next few pages are a sample of how my life was better from 1991 to 1996. Controlled mania has been more fun than controlled depression.

Now that my manic depression is less severe, more people at International Folk Dancing are friendly toward me. I have more smiles per hour.

I had a cashier job when I was depressed and also later when I was just a touch manic. Being a bit manic felt much better. When I was a bit manic, my coworkers were really warm and friendly. The customers were really friendly. I talked to customers just for the heck of it instead of only when absolutely necessary. I could cashier 40 percent faster with fewer mistakes. It was fun. During breaks from work, if I was in the bathroom, I also combed my hair instead of assuming that nobody was looking. When I did other jobs in the store, they seemed less baffling.

It used to really bug me when a customer would come up to me and say, "This will be cash."

I thought: *How annoying. Don't they know they don't have to say that? Don't they know that I don't care?*

When I was in a better mood, I thought nothing of it.

Music seems a lot more beautiful than it did when I was depressed.

Lately my apartment seems warm, friendly, and cozy. This is especially amazing because I only clean it twice as often. I bought seven new posters, new drapes, a new stereo, and I repaired holes in the wall.

I joined two Toastmaster's public speaking groups. Each group meets weekly, and for a couple of years I was president of one of the groups.

All of these happier feelings are because I'm stuck in a controlled mania instead of being stuck in a poorly controlled depression.

One of my coworkers at the store, Grace, was a really good friend. I've been overweight since 1984, so it is more difficult to keep my shirt tucked in. Being depressed, I just let my shirt out because I really didn't care. I figured nobody was looking. I figured life was such a tragedy that an untucked shirt really didn't matter. Anyway, one day she came to work with her shirt hanging out. It really looked stupid because she usually looked so nice. From then on I realized that I should tuck my shirt in or look stupid. From then on I kept my shirt tucked in whenever possible.

Grace did the same thing with table manners. Since becoming manic depressive, any table manners I had gradually deteriorated. Table manners seemed like a pointless ritual. Once, in the break room, Grace was eating something and then sucked the crumbs off of every one of her fingers. I thought, *Gee that's gross.* I wasn't used to seeing anyone else do that. Then I realized that everyone else was used to seeing me do that. I quit doing that. I started using napkins.

Feedback like that has helped me improve my appearance and manners.

I threw a thirty-sixth birthday party for myself in July of 1995. It was the first party I had thrown since 1972. There were about twenty-five people there.

I don't crack my knuckles as much anymore.

I have been going to more social events lately. I am friendlier and more outgoing than I was when I was depressed. I talk to my neighbors. I feel less difficulty going up to strangers and talking to them. I can tell people that I am manic depressive, if I feel like it. If I don't want to, I don't, but it is no big deal.

I've started playing poker again with a new group of friends that I met through International Folk Dancing.

In January 1997, after years of being on just antipsychotic Prolixin and side effect drug Cogentin, something even better came out. A new antipsychotic Zyprexa became available. I took it until 2013. It helped me sleep more soundly at night and stay more wide awake during the day. I took the Zyprexa at bedtime, and it put me to sleep. However, when I got out of bed in the morning, I didn't feel as hung over as I did on Prolixin. Life was easier by quite a bit. My mood stayed closer to normal most of the time. I was slightly depressed in the morning and slightly manic in the evening.

I was not completely healthy, but I was better than I had been for a long time. Every night before I went to bed, I looked to see what I had planned for the next day, and I often looked forward to the new day. That was much different than just hoping to cope with another annoying day. My plan since I was a little kid has always been to achieve maximum luxury. This doesn't mean riches; it just means feeling the best. I just want to have fun. I'm willing to work hard sometimes—or even a lot—but only if it is part of a plan to maximize fun. When I was depressed in the past, I had a difficult time even imagining how fun was possible. Now, with better medication, things are less complex and usually more fun.

CHAPTER 28

THE YEARS 1996–2013: BEING ALMOST OKAY

I finished writing the first version of this book in 1996, and it came out in 1997. I was proud of myself for getting the job done and for being the author of one of the very few autobiographies of type-one manic depressives. This book is one of only a few that describe the grandiose delusions and paranoid delusions of type-one mania. Manic depression is also known as bipolar affective disorder. There is manic depression type one and type two. The people who have type-two manic depression do not lose touch with reality. They do not get delusional when manic. They do get the other symptoms of mania, so it is still a problem sometimes. Both types get depressed badly at times.

There are actually many types of manic depression that do not really have names. It is known that a medication that works for one manic depressive might not work for another. Also, the side effects that manic depressives get from medication will often vary from person to person. There are many different types of individual brain chemistry and body chemistry.

They are also doing some genetic testing to help guess which medication will work best for each individual patient. This science is in its early stages but in the future might help determine what medication patients should try first. For now, medication choice is basically hit or miss.

In January 1997, I switched from antipsychotic Prolixin and side effect drug Cogentin to the new atypical antipsychotic Zyprexa. It controlled my chronic mania, and it had less of the side effect of muscle stiffness than Prolixin, so I didn't need the Cogentin. Zyprexa still had a low-interest-in-romance side effect like so many other medications, but not quite as bad as Prolixin. Zyprexa was better at making me sleepy at night and wider awake during the day. I took it at bedtime, and it put me to sleep for a full night's rest.

Around the year 2000, I got diagnosed with sleep apnea, so I got a CPAP machine. It helps me get a good night's sleep. Now I'm getting by on five or six hours of solid sleep, instead of ten hours of disturbed sleep. I have more time to work and play.

The antipsychotic Zypyrexa made my concentration good enough to get a job designing web pages in February 1997. I worked for a fairly large company that was mass-producing web pages for small businesses. We had about twenty telemarketers cold calling businesses to ask if they wanted a website to act as an online brochure or *Yellow Pages* advertisement. If a businessperson agreed to buy a website, the call was transferred to someone in my department, and we asked them what they wanted on their page. So, my job was to compose a couple of paragraphs to put on their site, after talking to them about what product or service they provided.

I held this job for four years until they laid off everyone in 2001 because they were losing money because our customers kept cancelling their pages. Their pages were not getting seen.

Of the twenty-five or so web page designers, I was the lowest ranking in quality and quantity of work. We were supposed to do twenty-two pages per day, and I usually did about fifteen. Also, our quality-control department often had to redo my pages because they did not meet company standards. My poor concentration and memory were still a handicap.

When I was laid off in 2001, I went back on Social Security disability and continued to get some money from my dad. I had more free time, so there were about five people I went out to lunch with monthly or weekly.

I spoke to local college psychology classes, reading excerpts from edition one of this book and taking questions. I continued to lead support groups at the Depression and Bipolar Support Alliance (DBSA) of Seattle.

At support groups, the topic of relationships often came up. There was often the question of why marriages go bad. Depression can cause trouble in relationships, but trouble in relationships can cause depression. Which came first—the chicken or the egg? It can sometimes take a mental health professional to help couples figure this out. The same cause and effect question is common at workplaces also.

Getting back to medication, I stayed on antipsychotic Zyprexa from 1997 until 2013. I started out on 5mg per day, and it gradually wore off, so I had to keep raising the dose. By 2013 I was on 50mg (20mg at 5 p.m. and 30mg at bedtime, which was usually about ten o'clock). The usual maximum recommended dose is 20mg per day, but Dr. Stark let me take more, up to 50mg per day. The medication was to control my chronic mania.

From 1997 until 2013, I often was on additional medications combined with the antipsychotic Zyprexa. These included antipsychotic Seroquel, mood stabilizer Lamictal, and mood stabilizer Tegretol. The goals were to stabilize mood, normalize sleep, and have a minimum of side effects.

Five different times during this period of 1997 to 2013, I noticed muscle twitches, and I was uncoordinated. I feared antipsychotic

Zyprexa was giving me tardive dyskinesia (TD), which causes muscle problems. TD is a long-term side effect of Zyprexa. The old-fashioned "typical" antipsychotics like Haldol are more likely to cause TD than Zyprexa, but Zyprexa can cause it too.

So, in an effort to prevent TD five different times, I switched to antipsychotic Clozaril, the only antipsychotic that does not cause TD. On just the Clozaril, the low-interest-in-romance side effect went away. All women looked more beautiful everywhere I went, all day, every day. When I saw married couples, I thought: *Wow! No wonder he likes being married to her!* Also, my muscles were much better, as predicted. I remember climbing the steps to the lab I had to go to to get the blood test you need for Clozaril. Climbing the steps was way easier. I thought: *Wow! I can run, swim, lift weights, and get thin again.* However, in spite of these two side effects being gone, the Clozaril made me very depressed instead of manic. On 50mg of Clozaril, I slept seven hours but woke up very badly depressed. It lowered my mood down from chronic mania into depression instead. Taking less than 50mg Clozaril would have made me sleep less than seven hours, which I considered unacceptable.

When I saw Dr. Stark and told him I was depressed, he said, "I'll give you an antidepressant."

Then, mistakes by me, all five times I said, "No thanks, I'll go back to the Zyprexa and Tegretol, or Zyprexa and Lamictal, or Zyprexa and Seroquel." (whichever combination I was on at the time).

I figured being on an antipsychotic, which brings my mood down, and an antidepressant, which brings my mood up, would be stupid. The main intended effects of the two drugs would counteract each other. They would cancel each other out, and both would give me side effects.

So, I went back to my combination of antipsychotic Zyprexa and whatever else I was on, in spite of the low-interest-in-romance side effect that they had. That was a mistake by me.

CHAPTER 29

MEREDITH

I met Meredith in 1987 at support groups for depressives and manic depressives. She went to the groups for moral support for her manic depression like me. The groups are now called Depression & Bipolar Support Alliance of Seattle, (DBSA of Seattle). She was a single mother and was the same age as me. She had first gotten depressed in twelfth grade, like I had. She went to a private Catholic high school in Seattle. We were both age twenty-eight when we met. We both spent some time volunteering at the DBSA office, answering phones, and doing some mailings to advertise the support groups.

She was bright, friendly, caring, and pretty, with long, straight shiny red hair. I spent some time hanging out with her, but at this time we were just friends. I had the low-interest-in-romance side effect from antidepressant Asendin.

In December, 1987 she married a guy, and I was a guest at her wedding. Then she moved out of state. She occasionally visited Seattle, and we would go out to lunch. In the year 1999 she got divorced and moved back to Seattle.

She called me up and said that she was divorced and back in town. I said, "Oh, Meredith, good hearing from you. Let's go out to lunch." She said, "Sure."

That was the start of our close friendship. We went out to lunch at Perkins, just as friends, almost every week, from 1999 to 2013. That's fourteen years.

Our typical conversation went something like this:

Meredith said, "Hi, how are you?"

I said, "I'm depressed and have the low-interest-in-romance side effect."

Meredith would always talk about her kids. She has a daughter Gertrude born in 1985 and a son Jacob born in 1991.

She would often say she was struggling with her mental illness and raising two kids on her own.

She often said, "I think I'm in a situational depression."

I often said, "It's probably from your chronic manic depression, not situational. Maybe increasing your medication dosage will help."

She usually said, "No. I think anybody in my situation would be depressed."

I usually said, "If we didn't have manic depression, any situation would feel better."

She sometimes dated.

I'd say, "Someday they'll invent better drugs, and the low-interest-in-romance side effect will go away. Then, you'll look pretty to me, like you do to most guys. Then we can be lovers, not just friends."

She said, "That would be good."

CHAPTER 30

UPDATE

Here is a letter I wrote to Dr. Haglund on November 25, 2015. She was my doctor from 1982 to 1988.

Hello Dr. Haglund,

Great news! I'm getting married to a woman named Meredith in May 2016!

We met at Washington Depressive and Manic Depressive Association (now DBSA) support groups in 1987. We went out to lunch at Perkins almost every week, just as friends, from 1999-2013. Then, there was a mixed blessing. I was diagnosed with Parkinson's Disease in November 2013. My combination of a huge dose of Zyprexa and Tegretol was replaced with Clozaril. Then, suddenly the "Low Interest in Romance" side effect went away and we became "More than just friends" on April 3, 2014.

The Parkinson's made me nearly quadriplegic for a while. They tried me on Sinemet for a few days, but I was so depressively pessimistic that when it did not work suddenly, dramatically, overnight the first night, I quit it. I was used to psych drugs like Haldol that work the first day or two. Then I had heard that electroconvulsive therapy was experimentally used for Parkinson's. So, reluctantly, I tried it weekly from September 2014 to June of 2015 (double sided, full strength). It actually worked very well for the Parkinson's but was of almost no help for my mood. However, I now consider the electroconvulsive therapy a big mistake because it caused horrible memory loss. I still can't remember how to get to the apartment I lived at in Kent, Washington for 12 years or so. To make a long story short, I've been taking Sinemet since June 2015 and it is working well for the Parkinson's. I take Clozaril at bedtime. It makes me sleep and it stops me from getting manic, but makes me depressed every morning, so I take Wellbutrin immediate release every morning and it cheers me up. This is the best I've been in years. [Wellbutrin has no "Low Interest in Romance" side effect.]

With great luck, I also read that Wellbutrin works for BOTH Parkinson's AND Depression. I found this out from the book "Psychiatric Nursing" by Mary Ann Boyd.

Just for the record, the antidepressant Asendin that I was taking from 1982-1988 is the worst antidepressant as far as messing with your Dopamine, and Dopamine problems are what causes Parkinson's, so I never should have been on it.

If you haven't already, read my book: Agents In My Brain, How I Survived Manic Depression, by my pen name: Bill Hannon, Open Court Publishing Company, 1997. All the names are changed. The first chapter,

"KGB Bloodhounds," is free on the internet at www.
manicdepression.biz

Let me know if you have film producer connections.
I'm writing a new edition of the book with the happy
ending of me and Meredith getting married.

I read on your web site that you coined the word
"bipolar." I hadn't known that. It sounds better than
"manic depression." Good idea.

I hope you are doing well. Please respond at your
convenience.

Sincerely,

Bill Hannon

APPENDIX A

SYMPTOM LIST

Here is the list of symptoms of mania and depression that psychiatrists, psychologists, general physicians, social workers, and laypeople should use to diagnose or recognize manic depression. People with the disease should be treated by a competent psychiatrist. My list comes basically from the booklet *Understanding Manic-Depressive Illness* (Clarke Institute of Psychiatry, Toronto, Canada). I have made some additions and substitutions and added some examples from my own experience, reading, and talking to others at support groups.

Mania (Being Manic)

1. Delusions of grandeur. This can be thinking you are God, Jesus, President, Beatle John Lennon, an FBI agent, King Tut, or thinking you have great powers, talents, or wealth. You are having a delusion when you jump to ridiculous conclusions from normal sights and sounds. This is not the same as a hallucination. For hallucinations, see symptom #10.

2. Paranoid delusions. These are unrealistic fears. This can include the thought that the devil, criminals, government, your doctor, boss, or spouse are out to get you. Note: Paranoia from being

manic can sometimes be confused with the pessimism of depression.

3. Reduced need for sleep. You may feel that you need very little sleep, and you may only sleep a couple hours a night. You may not sleep at all. You may be lying in bed concentrating on such big plans for the next day that you don't relax and sleep. You don't really mind the lack of sleep. This lack of sleep may be the only symptom you recognize in yourself.

4. Feeling very good. Except when experiencing paranoia, everything seems fun, and everything is more interesting. Colors seem brighter. Music sounds better. You are more talkative. Euphoria. This is the only disease where the sicker you are, the better you feel.

5. Rapid unpredictable emotional changes. You can switch from happy to angry quickly with no apparent reason. This can include yelling and screaming suddenly to the surprise of those around you.

6. Extreme irritability. You may get very demanding and get angry when people don't jump in response to your commands. You may get angry if they disagree with your delusions. You may get angry when people interrupt you, while you are coming up with what you think are great ideas.

7. Flight of ideas. When talking to people, you may jump from topic to topic. In your mind, there is a connection between these topics, but it is not clear to the listener.

8. Thinking everything is a clue directed to you. This includes thinking that dialogue and songs on the television, radio, or computer are being altered to give a special message to you. You also think that about newspaper articles and things strangers might say near you in public. You think the clues are secret

and most people don't notice them. The clues are usually words that have double meanings. You might think the clues are from God, Jesus, the Pope, the president, a dead relative, or from your favorite movie star.

9. Overspending. You may think you have great wealth or potential income, so you may spend or invest recklessly. You may give money away.

10. Hallucinations. Some people get visual, auditory, tactile, olfactory, or gustatory hallucinations. You are hallucinating when you are seeing, hearing, feeling, smelling, or tasting something that is not really there. You may or may not know that they are not real. When you get antipsychotic medication, the hallucinations will go away and you will probably realize that they were not real.

11. Hyperactivity. You may have so much energy that you go from one activity to another without stopping or thinking.

12. Increased sexual drive. Sexual indiscretions. You may want sexual intercourse many times a day, and you may pick up sexual partners indiscriminately. You may flirt outrageously.

13. Poor judgment. You probably won't recognize that you are ill. You are likely to refuse treatment and blame others for everything that goes wrong. You may drive recklessly. You will certainly say things that you shouldn't say, ask things that shouldn't be asked, and do things you shouldn't do.

14. Talking loud or fast.

15. Excessive phone calling, e-mailing, letter writing, texting, or posting on social media. You might try to contact people you know, used to know, strangers, famous people, or the whole world. Usually you want to tell these people of your great delusional plans. One woman tried to call the Pope to announce that she was the Messiah.

16. Excessive joking, punning or rhyming.

17. Excessive laughter.
18. Singing or dancing at inappropriate times.
19. Outrageous or unusual way of dressing to attract attention to yourself.

Depression

1. Sad, despairing mood.
2. Preoccupation with failures or inadequacies and a loss of self-esteem. You may think everyone outranks you. You may become obsessed with one negative thought and be unable to turn it off. Your mind is clogged with worries.
3. Feelings of uselessness. You feel you serve no purpose.
4. Feeling hopeless. You think things will never improve.
5. Excessive guilt. You might worry excessively that things you've done in the past were wrong, harmful, or illegal.
6. Slowed thinking, forgetfulness, difficulty in concentrating and making decisions. This is usually due to preoccupation with worries or hopeless feelings. The poor concentration makes it hard to do your job or schoolwork. You might think you are hard of hearing because you have trouble following conversation.
7. Nothing is fun. Loss of interest in work, hobbies, school, and people. Loss of feelings for family members and friends. Anhedonia.
8. Excessive concern about physical complaints. Feeling overwhelmed with the fear that you have some physical handicap or disease. You may or may not really have that handicap. Even if you do have that handicap, feeling unduly overwhelmed by a handicap may be a symptom of depression. You may know you have depression or manic depression and be preoccupied with that. You may excessively fear future mania or depression. This is often a sign that you are depressed right now.

9. Either agitation or loss of energy. You are so restless that you cannot keep still or are too tired and weak to do anything.

10. Changes in appetite and weight. This could be a big increase or big decrease in appetite and/or weight.

11. Sleep problems. You may sleep too little or too much. Often you cannot sleep because you are lying in bed, worrying about negatives too intensely to relax and fall asleep.

12. Decreased sexual drive.

13. Crying. Thinking about crying. Imagining yourself or other people crying. Or you may feel like crying but be unable to do so.

14. Irritability. You can be upset with everything and everybody around you. You don't like it when others interrupt your obsessive worrying, even if it is to say something nice, or you don't like what others have done in the past to you. Or, you don't like others to ask you to participate in things that used to be fun, but aren't fun now. This can come across as anger. You can be mad at everything and everybody who has helped you to reach this apparently awful occasion. On very rare occasions, this anger turns to violence.

15. Suicidal thoughts or actions. Suicide attempts.

16. The excessive use of alcohol or street drugs in an effort to self-medicate. Many manic depressives become chemically dependent. Then they have two diseases hurting them.

17. Loss of touch with reality. A few people get hallucinations when they are depressed. You are hallucinating when you are seeing, hearing, feeling, tasting, or smelling something that is not really there. You may or may not know that they are not real. When you get antipsychotic medication, the hallucinations will usually go away and you will probably realize that they were not real.

18. Psychomotor retardation. This means being uncoordinated. Taking a long time to do physical tasks. Slow movements. Clumsiness. Reduced athletic ability. It can even be hard to get up and get dressed.
19. Pessimism about the future. Fear of bad things that may happen in the future. Anxiety about upcoming events. Lack of confidence. Note: Pessimism from depression can sometimes be confused with the paranoia of mania.
20. Self-harming. Deliberately hurting oneself. Cutting yourself on purpose.
21. Compulsions. This might include knuckle cracking, nail biting, hand washing, pacing the floor, checking rituals, or other pointless repetitive actions.
22. Frowning not smiling.
23. Negativity. Taking everything the wrong way. If someone says something nice to you, you think they don't mean it, and that angers you. If they say something critical, you think they *do* mean it, and that angers you, too.

To qualify as manic or depressed, you usually need just four of these symptoms at the same time. There are normal depressions after a loss, but they should last only two weeks or so. If they last longer, treatment is recommended. The reader should also know that there are other diseases besides depression and manic depression that give the symptoms of depression. These conditions that seem like depression include side effects of birth control pills, side effects of blood pressure medication, thyroid disease, and hypoglycemia. The disease called "depression" is usually the cause of a prolonged low mood. However, you should get a complete physical examination soon after you start treatment with antidepressants, to rule out other diseases.

Appendix B

Resource List

Finding a Doctor:

To find a psychiatrist near you, ask your family physician for a referral or look up psychiatrists on line. You may also know someone who is a satisfied patient of a certain psychiatrist, so it may help to ask around. There is a serious shortage of psychiatrists in the United States, so you might be able to get good care from a nurse practitioner who specializes in mental health or from some other medical professional.

If you or someone close to you is suicidal, call your (or his or her) psychiatrist. If the person in question does not have a psychiatrist, call the suicide hotline in your area, or call 911.

Manic people will generally not recognize that there is something wrong with them the first time they are manic. If someone close to you is manic, call a psychiatrist, and follow the psychiatrist's instructions. If you are manic yourself, and you know it, call your psychiatrist and tell his or her secretary that it is an emergency. If it is after hours, call the emergency number. Or you may have standing orders from your psychiatrist to adjust your meds on your own, within a certain range.

If you are seeing a psychiatrist for a while and you are not getting much better, or if you just have to find an answer to a question that your doctor doesn't know, don't hesitate to get a second or third opinion. Switch doctors if that seems right for you.

For Support Groups and More Literature

For support groups and more literature about depression and manic depression, contact the Depression and Bipolar Support Alliance (DBSA) chapter nearest you. Support groups can help you learn about medications and provide moral support for you and your family. Members of support groups should feel free to recommend medication and dosage changes to each other, as long as it is clear that your doctor must also be consulted before you make a change. Minimizing symptoms and side effects is the name of the game.

Unnumbered Notes

Chapter 1

Edward R. Barnhart, ed., *Physician's Desk Reference*, 45th ed. (Oradell, N.J.: Medical Economics Data, 1991), 1896. Sinequan … hallucinations. Rare side effect.

Head East. "Save my life I'm going down for the last time." Never Been Any Reason. Head East, Flat as a Pancake, (A&M Records Inc. CS-3196, 1975).

Chapter 2

P. J. Clayton, C. Ernst, and J. Angst, "Premorbid Personality Traits of Men Who Develop Unipolar or Bipolar Disorders," European Archives of Psychiatry and Clinical Neuroscience 243 (1994): 340. There is a study that proves …

Chapter 4

John Born and James W. Jefferson, M.D., with assistance from the Lithium Information Center, *Lithium and Manic-Depression: A Guide,* booklet published by the University of Wisconsin (rev. January 1987), 10. Only 0.5 percent of the population gets the disease …

Chapter 7

Christine McVie, "Don't stop thinking about tomorrow" Don't Stop, Rumors, Fleetwood Mac (Warner 8413, 1977).

Felder, Henley, Frey "We are prisoners here of our own device" Hotel California. The Eagles (Asylum Records 45386, 1976).

Felder, Henley, Frey, "You can check out any time you like, but you can never leave." Hotel California, The Eagles (Asylum Records 45386, 1976).

Chapter 10

Shere Hite, "Lots of good information about lovemaking." *The Hite Report, A Nationwide Study of Female Sexuality*. Dell Publishing. 1976.

Chapter 14

O'Brian, "Let's do the time warp again." Time Warp. *Rocky Horror Picture Show* Soundtrack. (Rhino Records RI-70712)

Jimmy Page and Robert Plant. "If there is a bustle in your hedgerow, don't be alarmed now. It's just a spring clean for the May Queen … There walks a lady we all know, who shines white light and wants to show." Stairway To Heaven. Led Zeppelin IV. (Atlantic Records SD 7208)

Chapter 18

United States Pharmacopeial Convention, Inc., Drug Information for the Health Care Provider. "Asendin is the worst tricyclic antidepressant as far as one's sex life is concerned." (Rockville, Maryland)

Chapter 21

Mark S. Gold, M.D. with Lois B. Morris. "New antidepressants need to be tried for six weeks." *The Good News About Depression* (New York: Villard Books, 1987), 243.

Chapter 27

The Handbook of Psychotropic Agents. "Cogentin gets rid of some of the main tranquilizing, sedation effect of Prolixin." (Compendium Publications Group, Ltd., of Secaucus, New Jersey)

Chapter 30

Mary Ann Boyd. "Wellbutrin works for both depression AND Parkinson's." *Psychiatric Nursing, Contemporary Practice*, Enhanced Update, Mary Ann Boyd, 5th edition. (Wolters Kluwer), 155. Bupropion is generic Wellbutrin.

Appendix A: Symptom List

Mark S. Gold. "There are other diseases which give the symptoms of depression." *The Good News about Depression*, p. 77 (thyroid disease), 80 (cancer), 111 (birth control pills), 113 (blood pressure medications), 159 (hypoglycemia).

ACKNOWLEDGMENTS

I want to thank the following people for their countless hours spent reading and editing my book or performing other essential tasks.

Kathleen A. John A. Debra A. Gregory B. Ellen B. Joan B. Ann B. Miriam B. Donna B. Tom C. Brian C. Jack C. Marv C. Nancy C. Sara D. Ellen E. Colleen F. David F. Julie F. Sheila F. Olivia G. James G. Eve G. Lee H. Peggy J. Dana J. Sue K. Kate K. Frank K. Rick L. Mitch L. Herb M. Yvonne M. Ivan M. Wayne M. Kerri M. John M. Freda M. Carole M. Hank M. Liz M. Geena N. Sue N. Jody N. John P. Steve P. Rex P. Patrick R. Kitty S. Sue S. Harold S. William S. Peter S. Beth S. Aaron S. Denise T. Timothy T. John U. Ben V. Bruce W. Dave W. Larry W. Mary W. Joe W.

INDEX